THE 10 MOST ICONIC STORIE

MUST
KNOW
STORIES

ROBERT HARRISON

MUST KNOW STORIES by Robert Harrison
Published by Scripture Union, 207–209 Queensway, Bletchley, MK2 2EB, UK.
email: info@scriptureunion.org.uk
website: www.scriptureunion.org.uk

Scripture Union Australia: Locked Bag 2, Central Coast Business Centre, NSW 2252.
website: www.su.org.au

© Copyright Robert Harrison 2008

ISBN 978 1 84427 320 1
First published in Great Britain by Scripture Union 2008.

The right of Robert Harrison to be identified as author of this work has been asserted by him in
accordance with the Copyright, Designs and Patents Act 1988.

British Library Cataloguing–in–Publication Data: a catalogue record for this book is available from
the British Library.

Cover design and photography by Paul Airy of 4–9–0 Ltd, Wakefield
email: paul.airy@fourninezerodesign.co.uk

Internal design and typesetting by Creative Pages: www.creativepages.co.uk

Printed and bound in China by 1010 Printing International Limited

Scripture Union: Scripture Union is an international Christian charity working with
churches in more than 130 countries, providing resources to bring the good news about
Jesus Christ to children, young people and families, and to encourage them to develop
spiritually through the Bible and prayer. As well as coordinating a network of volunteers,
staff and associates who run holidays, church-based events and school Christian groups, SU
produces a wide range of publications and supports those who use the resources through
training programmes.

THE 10 MOST ICONIC STORIES FROM THE BIBLE

MUST KNOW STORIES

ROBERT HARRISON

'Every generation passes something of its values, heritage and stories onto the next. We rarely stop to think about it though ... it just happens ... somehow... from parent to child ... time and again. **Must Know Stories** gather timeless tales from the book that brings us God's story, made real from parent to child again. Pools of wisdom lie within. Enjoy soaking them up and passing them on.'

Alan Charter, Director, Children Matter!

'The values and virtues in these stories are transformational! Robert Harrison helps us recover our calling to be storytellers with positive impact on families and community.'

The Rt Revd and Rt Hon Richard Chartres, Bishop of London

For my godchildren:

Caroline, Nicholas, Rebekah, William, Katy, John, Stephen and Brigid

Once upon a time…

I was taking an assembly in a well-respected secondary school near my home. I had planned to tell the story of King Saul who, when hunting David to kill him, went into a cave to relieve himself – unaware that it was the very cave in which David and his fellow mercenaries were hiding.

I began my assembly saying, 'You know the story of David and Goliath…' and was met with a school hall full of blank faces.

I was surprised.

'Put up your hand if you know the story of David and Goliath.'

Worryingly few hands went up.

So I told the story of David and Goliath instead.

A few days later, through my door came an advert for a supermarket chain. It was a spoof of the David and Goliath story. How many people simply won't get the joke because they don't know the story? I wondered.

Not long after that, I heard a television news journalist employ the David and Goliath image in a piece about global computer giants. It was clear that although the reporter had heard of David and Goliath, he did not understand the story.

Next came a cartoon from a cricketing magazine, in which the diminutive David was accused of ball tampering.

Must Know Stories was born.

Scripture Union conducted research among school teachers and parents to find out which were the most culturally iconic stories in the Bible. The results were quite clear. These are the undisputed top ten must-know Bible stories.

Must Know Stories is not an attempt to promote Christianity. These stories are older than the Christian religion. Half of them come from the Jewish Scriptures, and a number have parallels in the Qur'an. These ten ancient, wonderful stories are worldwide cultural icons.

We conducted further research among young people in secondary schools to discover how well these amazing stories are known. The results were unsettling. Only the stories of Jesus' birth and death are widely known; the rest were recognised by only a minority of students. RE lessons focus on the practices and philosophies of different world religions; school assemblies are devoted to matters of discipline and general morality. Nobody seems to have noticed these remarkable tales of life and faith quietly slipping into obscurity.

Millions of young children encounter images of Noah and his colourful ark in toys, games and pictures. No FA Cup campaign is complete without references to David defeating Goliath. These stories fill our literature; they are repeatedly employed by journalists, politicians and cartoonists alike. But the knowledge of the stories themselves is rapidly fading.

It is a cultural tragedy.

Whether we are surveying Rembrandt's *Prodigal Son* or the sign outside the 'Adam and Eve' pub, if we do not know the stories, we are missing out.

There is only so much that a writer can do. I have lifted these stories out of the text of Jewish and Christian Scripture and presented them as stories about real people caught up in real struggles. They are stories about loss and pain, heroism and friendship, life and death. I hope that they find an echo in your own life and experience.

My task has been to retell these stories for your enjoyment, but that is only a beginning.

I urge you to join me in the greater task. After you have read these ten stories, please pass them on to others. Of course, the publishers would be delighted if you bought more copies of this book, but that is not important. What matters is that these stories are told, retold, and told again – until everyone knows them.

Robert Harrison

PS The stories are presented in this book in chronological order. If you are interested to know the order of importance indicated by our research, this is the *top ten*:

1　The crucifixion of Jesus
2　The birth at Bethlehem
3　Adam and Eve
4　The good Samaritan
5　The Ten Commandments
6　The prodigal son
7　Noah's ark
8　David and Goliath
9　Daniel in the lions' den
10　The feeding of the 5000

You will find translations of the original Bible text for these stories at the back of the book, starting on page 139.

MUST KNOW STORIES

Pages

1 **TO KNOW OR NOT TO KNOW** / ADAM AND EVE — 9

2 **IN THE DARK** / NOAH'S ARK — 23

3 **ORDER FROM CHAOS** / THE TEN COMMANDMENTS — 41

4 **A SMALL, SMOOTH STONE** / DAVID AND GOLIATH — 56

5 **A MAN YOU CAN TRUST** / DANIEL IN THE LIONS' DEN — 68

6 **FAMILY POLITICS** / THE BIRTH AT BETHLEHEM — 83

7 **AN IMPOSSIBLE REQUEST** / THE FEEDING OF THE 5000 — 96

8 **THE PARABLE OF JOSIAH AND TITCH** / THE PRODIGAL SON — 105

9 **TO TRAP A RABBI** / THE GOOD SAMARITAN — 115

10 **A MATTER OF DEATH OR DEATH** / THE CRUCIFIXION OF JESUS — 123

BIBLE TEXT

1 ADAM AND EVE — 139
2 NOAH'S ARK — 141
3 THE TEN COMMANDMENTS — 143
4 DAVID AND GOLIATH — 146
5 DANIEL IN THE LIONS' DEN — 148
6 THE BIRTH AT BETHLEHEM — 150
7 THE FEEDING OF THE 5000 — 152
8 THE PRODIGAL SON — 153
9 THE GOOD SAMARITAN — 154
10 THE CRUCIFIXION OF JESUS — 154

TO KNOW OR NOT TO KNOW

IT WAS AN old feeling. Not the feeling of being old; because he wasn't old and oldness was something he had never encountered. It was a feeling from the past, from before. If Adam had ever suffered from a cold – which he never had – it would have been akin to the feeling you and I get the day before we know we have a cold; that feeling of not really being ill, but not really being well. It was a feeling of not-quite-rightness, a feeling of incompletion. As he walked among the trees of his protected world that fateful morning, Adam felt… he felt as he had once felt before, though he had not known that he was feeling it at the time. He felt…

'Where is Eve?'

He had woken up and she was not there. That was not in itself unusual or uncomfortable. They were not a couple who needed to hold on to each other all the time. Such a need is rooted in fear, and Adam and Eve were as ignorant of fear as they were of old age. Sometimes they were together. Sometimes they were apart. They explored together and they explored alone. They lived as a couple and they lived as individuals. Their life, together and apart, was an uncounted now, an intense immediacy that was concerned neither with the past nor with the future. And that morning, among the timeless trees, Adam was…

'Where is Eve?'

You or I would have recognised the repetition. Eve was not there today; she had not been there yesterday. You or I would have counted; we would have counted back… counted back four, five, six days. We would have recognised the pattern. But Adam did not. In the eternal now in which he lived, there was no need to count; time had not yet distilled into numbers. Now was everything. Now was all that was needed. A now with Eve was always wonderful. A now without Eve was always heavy with the unarticulated hope of reunion, of the blending of two separate nows into a broader present. But this particular morning was different. The inarticulate hope for reunion had been replaced by a feeling of…

'Where is Eve?'

There had been a time, a time before, when there had been no Eve. It was a time when Adam slept and woke alone, and ate and drank alone, and ran and danced alone. He did not want to remember that time. Why would he? Eve was good. She was exquisite. She was all that he needed – and more. She was perfection made more perfect, joy made more joyous. She was full life made fuller.

'Where is she?'

Adam pulled a fresh fruit from the branch of a nearby tree. Before pressing it to his bright teeth he paused to name it. Adam named everything. He did not name things to classify them, to tie them into a previous experience, or restrict them into a determined future. For Adam, as for Eve, to name something was to give it meaning, to give expression to a moment of relationship. At this particular moment, the relationship was that between eater and eaten. He named the fruit. Whether he had ever eaten the fruit from that tree before, whether he had given it the same or a similar name if he had, he neither knew nor cared. The fruit looked good to eat. It smelled good to eat. It was good to eat. He named it, 'Good to Eat'.

Yet, at that moment, beneath that tree, on that uneasy morning, Adam felt that this particular fruit could have been better. It would have been better if he had been able to reach up his arm to twist down a second fruit and hand it to Eve. She would have named it too. They would have laughed. They would have merged their different names, played with them, sung them, danced them. And then she would have burst the fruit in her mouth, sending shining pips cascading down her breasts, and they would have laughed some more. Adam stood and looked at the denuded stalk in his hand and felt a need for more.

He reached up and took another fruit from the same tree. He brought it immediately to his teeth. No need to name this one.

'Where is Eve?' he asked the twittering forest.

This second fruit was less sweet, less succulent, less satisfying.

He tried another, and another, and another.

'Where is Eve?'

He considered to himself that there had to be another fruit on this particular tree that was as good as the first, the one that he had named Good to Eat. He climbed the tree to reach more fruit. He tried the largest. He tried the brightest. He tried the longest. He searched in vain.

His belly was full but his search was not ended. Would he have to eat every single fruit on the entire Good to Eat Tree?

'Where is Eve?'

He had had enough. He slid down through the branches and leapt easily to the forest floor. He felt an urge to walk, to walk swiftly.

So he walked.

The brush of soft ferns against his skin felt good. But it didn't make him dance. It always made Eve dance. And Eve's dancing was an invitation Adam could never refuse. She would crouch and stretch and jump and slide, relishing the subtle sensations of the fern against all the different areas of her smooth flesh.

Adam walked.

'Where is Eve?'

The forest track brought him out into the open, into the sun's heat. He walked on. There was a great deal of walking to be done that morning. A herd of horned creatures browsed contentedly on the sunlit grass. Adam shouted them a name. They looked up, acknowledged their namer with a shake of their sleek heads, and returned to the business of eating.

Eve would have rushed among the herd, embracing necks, caressing flanks, engaging eyes. She was like that.

Adam walked on, stepping deftly round a lark who had built her nest on his path. The lark sang as Adam passed. But her song failed to thrill.

The feeling of not-quite-rightness pervaded the morning. The forest was a touch too cool; the sun a fraction too hot. The grazing herd had been too far away for Adam to choose to visit it; the lark too close.

Where was Eve?

'Eve?'

'Eve!'

Only the distant lark replied.

Adam had to get to the place he was walking towards: the particular place, the place in the very middle, at the very top; the place where he found meaning.

This particular place was a tree. This particular tree always had fruit, and its fruit was always fresh. It was a centre of reference in the constantly changing life of the forest. It was a place that made sense. At this tree, beneath its shade, all the complex references of Adam's existence found order. This one tree, unlike everything else that lived in the forest, had a single unchanging name – 'Knowing'. It was the tree of knowledge. And that morning Adam needed knowledge. He needed to know where Eve was.

At last he arrived at the centre of all that he knew, at the tree he called Knowing.

Adam leaned against its reassuring trunk and closed his eyes. With his flesh there, resting against the rounded bark, he let his jumbled accumulation of experience take order.

He was alone.

He was in the forest without Eve.

He was at the Knowing Tree without Eve.

They had been here together.

They had been here together many times.

It was here that they had first explored their differences and made sense of them.

It was here that longing had flowered into love.

It was here that he had first met Eve on a bright, fresh morning. What a morning that had been! What joy! What completeness! What a dance they had danced together, the fusion of likeness and otherness.

At the Knowing Tree, these shards of knowledge came together and formed a meaningful pattern.

It was here that the Creator had given Adam the knowledge that having another someone to share life with would be better than all the wonder of being alone in the forest. And the Creator had been right. On that barely remembered night, Adam had gone to sleep alone at the Knowing Tree and had woken up to find Eve by his side. What a find! The Creator had said to him, 'She is very good.' And the Creator had been right.

Here at the Knowing Tree, this new... this uneasy morning, Adam smiled. He smiled deeply. He smiled for the first time since he had woken alone.

He looked up into the branches of the tree and saw its fruit. That fruit gave meaning to every other fruit in the forest. It was the fruit of Knowing. Looking at that fruit, Adam knew that he could eat any fruit that he desired in all of the rest of the world. The fruit of that one tree was the template of goodness. Any fruit that in any way resembled it was good. Any fruit that bore no resemblance to it was not good – not for him nor for Eve. He knew that. He knew it because the tree in the centre of everything was the tree of the knowledge of goodness – a gift from the Creator. And he also knew that he should never eat the fruit of that tree. The Creator had told him so. It was fruit for knowledge, not for eating.

'Where is Eve?'

Adam closed his eyes again and let his knowledge take order. He followed his thoughts as his eyes had just followed the branches of the Knowing Tree, from their fruit-laden tips to its sturdy centre. His mind led him back to the moments when there had been no Eve. They were not moments when Eve was elsewhere enjoying the aloneness of life. They were moments when Eve had not been... moments when there had just been him, Adam, and the other creatures he loved to name.

Leaning against that unmoving tree, Adam's feelings found their point of resonance. They echoed back to him from his long-stored past. Through all his and Eve's uncounted days of togetherness and apartness, Adam had not known this morning's feeling. But he had known it before, long before, before Eve, before duets and harmonies and pas de deux.

Leaning against the Knowing Tree, Adam found the knowledge he was searching for.

He was lonely. He was lonely… again.

Adam suffered a new feeling. It was a feeling you and I know very well, but which – for Adam – was entirely new. It was a feeling of heaviness, of slowness, of dullness. It was as though the colour of the forest, with all its fruits and flowers, had been subtly dimmed. It was as if the singing of the lark had diminished and the squawk of the crows had grown deafening.

Adam was sad.

'Where is Eve?'

The Knowing Tree had led Adam to knowledge but it was not a comfortable knowledge. It was a knowledge that made him run. But it wasn't a running that was exhilarating. It wasn't running in the way that he and Eve would run among the antlered herds in the cooling evening. This was urgency. Adam knew urgency, the compulsion to do something quickly. He knew the urgency of finding a refreshing stream after a day wandering the Dry Lands. He knew the urgency of finding a place to sleep after a long evening of dancing beneath the silent moon. He also knew that essential urgency, that opposing urgency from the need to eat: the urgency to crouch and empty himself. This new urgency was akin to that. It was something that had to be done, though there was no particular delight in doing it. He had to find Eve, and he had to run to find her. If he had ever before known fear or dread, as you and I do, he would have known that feeling. But he did not.

'Eve!'

'Eve?'

This feeling was new. The tree that had so often led Adam to the knowledge of goodness had led him to an other knowledge: a knowledge of closing rather than opening, of ending rather than beginning.

'Eve!'

Adam passed a startled creature which scuttled out of his path to avoid collision. He did not pause to name it; it would not have been a pleasant name if he had. He had to find Eve. Somehow, in the flood of compulsion, he understood that this day was not a day for meeting new creatures. It was a day for being with Eve.

He spotted a ripe fruit, fallen on the path ahead of him. It needed to be eaten; it was there to be eaten. Adam could not resist the impulse to name the fruit; he called it 'Eat Me'. But the urgency to find Eve was stronger than the need to honour the falling of the fruit. He ran on, the Eat Me fruit collapsing under the weight of his foot.

He could feel the fruit's sweet flesh clinging to his skin as he mixed it with the earth of the forest floor. This urgent day, he pondered, was like the squashing of that fruit.

'Eve?'

'Eve!'

Adam crashed through a deep stream, scattering speckled fish. He ran down and down, down and away, down and outwards. Then he came to a division in the path. Which way should he go? Every time he had come to a parting of ways before, it had not mattered. All paths led to succulent fruit, to fresh water and carefree animals. Whether he was with Eve or alone, all paths were good paths. But now it mattered. All paths were no longer equal. One led to Eve, the other did not. How could he know which? At such times Adam always made his way to the Knowing Tree. There he could perceive the deeper patterns that governed the lives of all the creatures the Creator had made. But this day he was running away from the tree. He knew the way to the tree. The way to the tree was up, and in. He was heading out.

'Eve?'

'Eve?'

He had stopped at the parting of the ways. He looked one way, then the other. Then he looked behind him. There was a third way there: it was a way he had never taken before, neither he nor Eve. They had never gone back, they had never needed to. Now Adam looked back.

They had slept side by side during the night. Should he go back to where he had last known her? There seemed no more reason for going back than there was for going to the left or to the right. He was lost. Lost… not so much in location as in purpose. He had to find Eve, but how could he find her?

'Eve!'

'Eve!'

He sat on the path and waited. He was waiting for knowledge. He had always visited the Knowing Tree when he needed knowledge, but now he waited for knowledge to come to him. It was not a foolish thing to do. The tree was only a sample of knowledge, a symbol of it. True knowledge came from the Creator and the Creator might be encountered at any place and at any moment. So, on that morning, this particular parting of the ways was as good a place as any for Adam to wait.

'Adam!'

'Adam?'

Adam was on his feet in a moment. He knew that voice. It was the voice of joy and love and completeness. It was a voice that always excited him, that caused his heart to pump harder and his body to grow fuller.

'Eve!'

Eve came crashing down the path towards him. There was a look about her that Adam had seen before but not in his beloved Eve. It was the look he had seen in the face of the unnamed creature which had scurried out of his way earlier that day.

Eve stopped and bent over, struggling for breath. She was dripping water… not water from the stream, nor from the rain. It was water than clung to her forehead and dribbled down her cheek.

This was different.

'Where have you been?' They both spoke at once.

Adam was first to answer their shared question. 'I have been looking for you.'

'I have been looking for you,' Eve reported.

'You were not there when I woke,' Adam said to his companion. 'But today is a day for being together.'

'I had to meet the Clever One,' Eve explained.

'Who is the Clever One?' Adam enquired.

His question came with yet another new feeling. He was having a day of new feelings. He felt that he didn't like this Clever One. This Clever One seemed, to him, like a large, slow creature getting in your way when you are dancing. Adam wished very strongly that Eve had not left him in the early greyness of that morning in order to converse with this Clever One. He repeated his question, and with passion: 'Who is this Clever One?'

'A creature,' Eve replied evasively.

'What creature?'

'There are so many.' She did not look at Adam as she spoke. This was different as well. 'I'm not sure I can remember the names we have given it.'

Adam felt a need to repeat himself. This was new too. Their life of eternal now had been a never-ending, never-repeating pattern of goodness. But now he was forced to repeat himself, and it felt like the repeating of the dissatisfying fruits of that morning's meal.

'What creature?'

'I'll take you to him,' Eve offered.

'How will you find him?' Adam asked. He had never looked for a particular creature before. He and Eve had just enjoyed those they encountered as they explored the world together.

'He is always in the same place,' Eve explained. She knew more of this creature than she was admitting.

The woman set off… turning back the way she had come.

They walked. There was no dance in Eve's step; she just walked… up the hill, labouring for breath. Adam followed. He did not walk beside her because Eve was walking ahead. So they did not clasp hands or hold shoulders or enfold waists. They walked separately. And Eve talked. She did not talk with Adam. She just talked.

'I met him some days ago. He was waiting for me on the path. He told me how beautiful I was and then began to tell me how much more beautiful I could become. He is very clever. He knows all about the forest. He knows about the Knowing Tree. He knows the Creator as well. He says that there are many kinds of things that we could know that the Creator has not told us. He says that the Creator does not delight in knowledge, and that is why he told us not to eat the fruit from the Knowing Tree.'

She continued to talk. She did not stop talking. It was more than Adam could grasp. He struggled to listen in the same way that Eve struggled to climb the hill. Adam watched as the clinging water seeped out of the smooth skin of her back. He needed to visit the Knowing Tree. He needed to understand all that was happening.

They came to a parting of the way. One path led upwards towards the Knowing Tree, the other did not. Eve took the second path. Adam paused for a moment. He wanted to continue upwards, to find some order in his muddle. But he also wanted to stay with Eve; today was a day for being together. As he looked along the upward path he felt a longing for some light to shine into his inner gloom. As he looked along the path that Eve had chosen he felt a need not to be alone in the darkness.

He followed Eve.

They came to a clearing beside a tree that bore a fruit that was not good to eat. It was not at all like the fruit of the Knowing Tree. It was hard and brown. Some creatures ate this fruit, he knew, but it was no good for him and Eve. Nonetheless, this was where she had stopped.

'He isn't here,' Eve said.

Adam peered up into the branches.

'What does he look like?'

'He is long and slender,' Eve described, 'with short legs and broad feet. His skin is brightly patterned with shining scales. He is not like any other creature.'

'Is he the one we once called Serpent?'

'I do not remember.'

Adam knew that she did remember. Her wandering eyes informed him.

This was different.

Adam looked around. This clearing was a good place for dancing. But he did not feel like dancing. He felt like running, like running upwards, up to the centre. But he did not wish to be apart from Eve. So he stayed.

'He is always here,' Eve explained. 'Every morning, every day… I don't understand.'

There was a silence, an uncomfortable silence.

Eve began to pull up some of the small yellow and white flowers that grew among the grasses of the clearing, collecting them into a pile.

Adam watched and wondered.

This was different.

He needed to return to the Knowing Tree to find understanding of these things. But he mustn't leave Eve. He leaned against the tall, straight tree and searched for a meaningful pattern among his thoughts. All the while, he watched Eve.

Eve kneeled beside her heap of broken plants, taking each in turn and making a slit in their thin green stems with her fingernail.

This was different.

That done, she began to thread the stem of one small flower through the slit in the stem of another. She repeated this, assembling the flat, round flowers with their short, straight stems into a single strand of white, yellow and green.

Adam watched. But he could find no meaning in Eve's actions.

When she had placed all of the flowers – Adam named them 'Little Suns' – into her strand, Eve attached the first Little Sun's stem to that of the last, thus making a soft loop. She held her handiwork up for him to see, and she smiled. Adam did not look at the twisted flowers, he looked at the smile. It was good to see Eve smile; it was wonderful. It thrilled him. It was good for them to be together.

Eve lifted her loop of Little Suns and guided it carefully over her head, bringing it to rest on her shoulders and against her breasts.

'You see,' she said, her voice clear and strong. 'It makes me more beautiful. The Clever One said it would.'

And with that she began to dance. She danced around the Clever One's tree with its dark, uneatable fruit. But Adam did not feel invited into this dance. This was a solo. It was a strange dance, an exclusive one. He looked at the loop of fading flowers she had made. It looked to him as a pair of heavy tusks would look on a rabbit or as a bright bunch of curved yellow fruit would look on a delicate climbing rose.

At last, standing beneath the tree that was not the Knowing Tree, Adam found the knowledge that he needed: this was not good.

He stepped forward to leave… to leave alone… to go where he wanted and needed to go – to the Knowing Tree.

Eve was still dancing. She whirled towards him, stopped right in front of him and threw herself onto him, embracing him wildly. Adam stepped back to keep his balance. His arms remained at his side. This was not a shared embrace like the one they had enjoyed under the Knowing Tree on their first morning together. This embrace was not good either.

Adam fell back onto the grass. Eve landed on top of him, legs astride him, her face drenched with sweat.

'Where were you going?' she demanded. She did not wait for him to reply, but added, 'I need you.'

Adam grasped Eve's arms, to push her away.

Eve resisted, leaning forwards against him. But Adam prevailed; he was taller and stronger. Eve rolled backwards through the deflowered grass and Adam jumped swiftly to his feet.

This was a strange dance. It was not good.

'I'm going to the Knowing Tree', he stated firmly, and set off.

'Oh, good,' Eve replied. 'I'll come with you.' She skipped along to join him.

'That's where we need to go,' Eve explained delightedly, snaking her arm around Adam's.

He walked on. He had resolved to go to the Knowing Tree with or without her.

'The Clever One told me all about it,' she said. 'We both need to eat its fruit.'

'If we eat the fruit from the Knowing Tree, we will die,' Adam said confidently. Somehow, the limitless fascination that Eve once held for him had ended. At that moment he had no interest in her. He only wanted to get back to the centre, to the top, to the place where things had a pattern and a purpose. 'The Creator told us that,' Adam continued. 'He knows about these things.'

'But we won't die,' Eve insisted.

'He said we would.' Adam was emphatic. His heart was pounding, not from the effort of climbing, but from the challenge of their disagreement.

'The Clever One said we wouldn't die.'

'The Creator said we would.'

They had never spoken like this before. It was different, and it was not good.

Eve disengaged herself from Adam's arm and skipped ahead a few paces, allowing Adam a brief moment of relief. She stopped a short distance up the path, and stood there, legs wide, arms wide, smile wide, a picture of vitality.

'Look,' she beamed. 'The Clever One was right. We won't die. I didn't die. I ate the fruit of the Knowing Tree this morning and here I am, as alive as you are!'

Adam froze. He stared. Eve was looking directly at him. She was telling him truth. She had eaten the Knowing fruit. She had not died. Or had she? What did it mean: 'to die'? Adam realised that he did not know. At the Knowing Tree – before – when the Creator had told him about the fruit, he believed he knew what 'to die' meant; it was something unnecessary; it meant to be without purpose; it was to be both unloved and unlovable. Is that what had happened to Eve? Is that why he no longer wanted to dance with her?

But he did want to dance with her. He wanted to dance as they had danced before, thrilling with the excitement of the moment and the delight of otherness.

In all his confusion, Adam grasped a reality: he wanted to be with Eve. It was not good for a man to be alone. The Creator had said that to him and the Creator knew about these things. Or did he? The Clever One knew about these things too.

Adam marched on, up the hill, passing Eve. She ran after him. She was talking. He wasn't listening. But that didn't stop her from talking. And the more Eve talked, the less Adam listened.

At last he came to the top, to the middle, to the Knowing Tree. He flopped against it, embracing it with both arms, desperately soaking in its unchanging familiarity after a day of relentless innovation. Adam closed his eyes tightly and allowed the events of the morning to take their places in his mind.

He had woken alone, without Eve – and that was not good, though he had not known it at the time.

Eve had stolen away to meet the Serpent. That had not been good either.

The Knowing Tree had never led Adam to such bad knowledge before. It tired him intensely, but he had to keep working at it.

What was Eve up to now? Adam did not know.

Ever since he had woken, he had felt that something was not good. That's why he had come to the Knowing Tree for the first time that day. That was a good thing to do.

At the Knowing Tree, he knew that he had to find Eve. So he searched for her. But he failed to find her. He failed to find her because she had gone back and he had gone forwards. Then he had stopped searching and waited, and Eve had found him.

The rest of his memory of the day was fresh – fresh and raw.

Where was Eve?

'Adam.'

Her voice came from above him, from up in the tree.

'I'm up here,' she called.

He looked up. Eve was perched among the branches, eating. She was eating the fruit from that same tree, the fruit that was for Knowing and not for eating.

Or was it?

'Eve, stop!' Adam shouted urgently.

'It's delicious,' Eve slurped, the fruit's orange juice dripping down her arms, chin and breasts.

'If you eat that, you'll die!'

'Don't be silly. If we eat it, it will give us knowledge; it is the fruit of knowledge. That's what the Clever One told me: we will become like the Creator. Oh, Adam, won't it be wonderful to be like the Creator? He knows so much.'

'I don't want to know.' Adam turned away.

'Of course you do.'

She was right. If he had not wanted to know, he would not have looked back up to her. But he did.

'I'll tell you what I know, Adam.' Eve was dripping with knowledge as much as the fruit in her hand was dripping with glistening juice. 'I know how you are feeling. You are feeling scared. You have not felt it before today, but you are feeling it now. You are scared of losing me, Adam. You are scared of me knowing things that you don't. You are scared of the Clever One, because he told me things that you didn't know. You need this fruit, Adam. You need the knowledge that it will give you. Here.'

Carelessly she plucked the nearest fruit and dropped it to him. He caught it. It was smooth and waxy, a blend of red, green and yellowy orange. Adam looked at it. His body was tingling with excitement. The excitement was very much like all the other joys he had known, but subtly different. This excitement was flavoured with fear. Excitement, as Adam had known it before, was a feeling that followed something. It followed the exuberance of dancing; it followed the crimson sunrise; it followed an embrace with Eve; or the arrival of the Creator. This familiar excitement was always a response… a reaction. But the new excitement was an anticipation of something that had not… yet… happened.

'Eat it!' Eve called cheerfully from above.

At that moment, the Creator's voice echoed from Adam's memories: 'You must not eat the fruit from this one tree. It is for Knowing. On the day that you eat it, you will surely die.'

It did look good to eat.

Adam had never touched this fruit before. And now that he did it seemed all the better to eat. It had a softness that other large fruits lacked, but it also had a firmness not found in the berries of the forest. It did look very good to eat.

'Eat it,' Eve repeated. She was climbing down to him.

Adam fought to understand the fear-tinged excitement he was experiencing. He wanted to eat it, but also he didn't want to. The Creator had said, 'Don't'. The Clever One had said, 'Do'. The Creator had said, 'You will surely die'… but what did that mean? Was Eve dead? It didn't seem so. The Clever One had said, 'You will be like the Creator.' Surely the Creator wasn't dead!

Eve swung down from a branch and landed heavily. There were red lines on her thigh and some of the lines seeped beads of dark red water. She walked unevenly towards him.

This was different.

Her face was smothered with the sticky orange juice. She clutched the half-eaten, ragged remains of a Knowing fruit.

'Eat it,' she commanded. 'It's the best ever.'

Adam looked again at the fruit in his hand. Once again his body flushed with the excitement of the unknown.

'I know what you're feeling,' Eve explained. 'You're worried. You're worried that everything will change if you eat it.'

Now that she said it, Adam knew that Eve was right.

'Well, it will and it won't,' Eve continued. 'Look at me. I'm the same me, but I know things.'

Adam's gaze was drawn to the trickle of redness running down his companion's leg.

'What's that?'

'It's nothing,' Eve dismissed. 'Just a scratch.'

She did know things. She knew things that he didn't. How foolish of him not to know a scratch when he saw one. The Clever One was right: Eve had become like the Creator. This knowledge was appealing. He wanted more of it.

'What about that?' Adam asked, pointing to a small flat creature lying on the ground behind Eve. It had not moved since the moment Eve had swung down from the tree.

Eve turned and bent down to study the creature.

'It's dead,' she announced. 'I must have landed on it when I jumped down. But it doesn't matter.'

It did to Adam.

He crouched by the flattened beast. It too had seeped red liquid. He prodded it with his finger. It did not respond. So this was death. The Clever One had been right. Eve had eaten the forbidden fruit and she was not dead.

Adam had placed his fruit on the ground in order to prod the dead creature. Eve picked it up and presented him with it.

'Eat it, Adam.'

It was like the parting of the way where he had stopped earlier. He had to eat the fruit, or not eat it. Instinctively he turned and looked behind him. But there was no going back. That he knew. He could eat the fruit and embark on the fearful excitement of an unknown future, or he could leave the fruit and be alone again.

That was the issue. Eve had already chosen. She had taken the path of knowledge. She knew all about fear and worry and scratches and death. And she was hungry for more.

Standing in front of her, Adam felt small, as he felt when beneath a vast tree; he felt slow and weak.

A surge of emotion flooded through him. He would not settle for that. It was right for him to be bigger than Eve, to be stronger, to be faster... to be more clever. The fruit would bring him that.

He reached out and took it from Eve's hand.

'Eat it,' she smiled, looking directly into his eyes.

Adam knew something else. Eve was wonderful. He cast his eye over her beautiful body. It excited him. If he didn't follow Eve, he might lose her.

Eve shifted uneasily under Adam's gaze. She moved her empty hand to cover the part of her body he was looking at. This was different. She had never done that before. Adam did not understand it, but he expected that Eve did.

She turned away from him and skipped awkwardly to a nearby tree, a tree which had green-black fruit and broad leaves. She tore down two large leaves and held them over the parts of her that Adam was studying innocently. The juice-drenched skin of her face flushed hot red.

This was different too.

The feeling of dread that had accompanied Adam since the moment he woke that morning deepened.

If he didn't follow Eve, if he didn't eat the fruit resting in his hand, she might abandon him for her new knowledge... and he would be alone again. But it was not good for a man to be alone – the Creator had said that. The Creator knew about these things. And Adam now knew that if he ate the fruit, he would know about these things too.

He looked into Eve's knowing eyes. He looked at the motionless, lifeless creature at his feet. He looked up into the fruit-laden branches of the Knowing Tree. He looked at the firm, smooth, green-orange-red forbidden fruit in his hand.

And he ate it.

IN THE DARK

APPROACHING STORM

'NOAH!' Jenaia's voice pierced every corner of the complex wooden structure. Instantly, all four men, in their different locations, stopped what they were doing and looked up. They would have heard that voice if a herd of antelope was clattering past at the same time. The voice of wife and mother is deeply imprinted in the conscience of every man.

Each of them, at their own task, had been working feverishly all day to get as much as possible done before this moment. Now their time was up; their crime had been discovered. Noah placed his heavy wooden mallet carefully on the floor. Then he mopped the sweat from his face. There was just time left for him to feel satisfied at a good day's work.

'NOAH!'

She had found him. The shrivelled but sturdy form of his wife came in view. He could make out the bright colours of his three daughters-in-law huddled together in the background.

'Ah, there you are, my love.'

Jenaia was not distracted from her fury by the shallow sympathy on her husband's face.

'Where – in the name of all that is good – is my bronze cooking pot?'

Noah had known he would have to weather a storm for the appropriation of his wife's most prized possession, but he had judged that the lashing of her tongue presented a lesser danger than the actual storm which he and his sons were labouring, every waking hour, to escape.

'Shem and Ham have it, dear, up on the top deck.' His voice and his manner were tired. His tiredness, unlike his sympathy, was utterly genuine. Noah knew that it was a coward's reply, but he also knew that his wife would moderate her fury when applying it to her sons.

'I shudder to imagine what they might be doing with it,' the long-suffering matriarch declared. She turned and plodded away with determined steps.

Noah allowed himself the slightest hint of a smile beneath his ancient beard, and mouthed silently, 'You could never, in your worst nightmares, imagine what they are doing with your precious pot.'

Ignorant of her husband's words, the sun-dried mother made her way towards one of the many ladders serving Noah's mammoth boat. She was fit, for her considerable age.

'I don't suppose you are going to tell me what they're up to, are you, Noah?' she said pointedly, without turning round. She knew better than to wait for an explanation.

'They're sawing wood with it, my dear,' he muttered, confident that his wife was out of earshot.

Noah and his sons would never have dared do what they had done when their wives were at home. But the women had been away and the men urgently needed some metal tools. They had considered numerous other sources for the rare and costly bronze, but Jenaia's cooking pot was readily available and – from all the love that their womenfolk bestowed on it – wonderfully clean. This very expensive item was just what they needed.

They had spent most of the previous night building a furnace to melt the thick metal, and shaping moulds into which to pour it. After their brief snatch of sleep, the new tools were cool and ready for use. And they were wonderful. Exactly what was needed. They needed the speed and accuracy which only metal gave. Their deadline was not negotiable; come the spring rains, the real storm would begin. On that day there would only be two options: float or drown.

'AAAAH!'

Jenaia had found out.

Noah had his explanation prepared. He had been working on it all night and all day. His had been no act of rash vandalism, though that was increasingly common in those days. It was a matter of lifesaving necessity. It had been with grave faces and heavy hearts that the four men had flattened and melted the gleaming cauldron. Each knew too well the trouble they would get from their wives. But it had to be done.

Noah listened to the creak and clatter of his wife making her way back to the lower deck of his boat. He had not resumed work during her absence. He had prayed. He prayed to the God of his ancestors: the God who had created the world and who sustained all life; the God who had resolved to wipe out the violence and selfish indifference of the current age; the God who had instructed Noah to build this monstrous boat; the God who had determined to send spring rains that would last well into the summer and destroy every living creature in the known world. Those rains were only a few months away now. Noah and his sons simply had to have metal saws if their boat was to be ready in time.

He rehearsed these thoughts towards his Creator while his wife's dogged footsteps descended the complex series of steps and walkways.

Then there was silence.

What was she up to? Noah strained his ears. He could pick up no clue. He began, hurriedly, to review his assumptions about how Jenaia might respond. Her silence was unnerving. She was a shouter, not a sulker.

Without warning, the woman who had been Noah's faithful companion for more years than he cared to count stole into the lower store chamber, her footfall catlike, her face pale… the eye of the hurricane. She stood a while, motionless. There was not an agitated twitch about her. Noah had never seen his wife so still; he had never seen her so angry.

He drew breath to speak, to begin his explanation, but said nothing. Every scenario for this encounter that he had rehearsed over the past day was a response to a furious tirade. He was ready for shouting, he was ready for insults, he was ready for the resurrection of long-forgotten failings. But he was not prepared for this.

Finally, she spoke, with a voice as gentle as a doe's.

'Why?'

Noah stepped forward to embrace his wife, to reassure her that even though he had destroyed her most valued possession, he still loved her.

She held out an age-worn arm to prevent him. That wrinkled arm could not have felled hundreds of mature trees, using only flint axes, as Noah and his sons had done; that arm could not have pulled on rough ropes to raise entire tree trunks high into the air, as his own arms had, day after day, month after month; but – to Noah – Jenaia's lean arm was as powerful as a lion's paw.

He obeyed it.

Noah had bought the bronze cauldron for Jenaia shortly after he started work on his astounding boat. It was a reassurance of his love for her, a gift to make her life easier and placate her while he and their sons were away felling timber. The purchase had cost him a great weight of valuable grain and dried fruit, but he had deemed it necessary. It is not easy for a woman to accept that her husband has been in conversation with an unseen and unseeable God, or that he has been instructed to construct a floating farmyard larger than any of the strange temples dominating the local settlements. The bronze cauldron was the ideal gift. Not only was it fundamentally useful, but it also assured Jenaia that her husband valued her above all his unfashionable principles and opinions.

Noah vehemently disliked bronze and all that the innovative metal had done to the world in which he lived. Bronze may have made tools more efficient, but it also made weapons more deadly. There had always been scuffles between rival settlements, but in the days before bronze these had ended in bruises; now they ended in bloody death. It was much easier to hunt deer with bronze-tipped spears and arrows. Hunting parties returned from their work with twice as much game as before. This had heralded an era of more frequent and more indulgent parties, but while people's bellies had grown fatter, the forests had become disturbingly empty. As hunters were forced to travel further and further afield, violent clashes between tribes became commonplace. This new era of convenience and plenty facilitated the age-old habit of human greed. Noah did not trust bronze.

Throughout his construction project, he had doggedly made do with traditional flint tools. But now, time was against him. Winter was approaching and they had only just begun work on the ark's roof. Shem had repeatedly stated that they could not finish in time without the new technology. They had debated the matter for weeks.

'Father,' Japheth had added, 'don't blame the metal; the fault lies with the people who misuse it.'

Noah was still not convinced. Ham joined the argument. Without bronze tools, they would all be destroyed by the coming storm, he said.

Japheth had come up with the clinching sentence: 'Father, it is not the Creator's will for you to drown in this flood.'

Then, two nights ago, when the women were away, Noah decided to sleep in the ark, beneath the small area of newly completed roof. It had rained in the night. The modest pile of dry straw on which the old man was sleeping quickly became sodden. Rainwater poured through gaps where splintered timbers could not hold up the wet thatch. As Noah lay there – wet, cold and miserable – he knew that bronze tools would have produced stronger joints in a fraction of the time.

Time was the key issue. They did not have time to get everything perfect, neither did they have time to travel to the mountains and negotiate terms with the bronzesmiths. Instead, the women were away, the prized pot was there… enough good quality bronze to make straight saws and sharp chisels. They worked magnificently.

Noah looked at his wife. She was as still as death.

'If we manage to get this boat ready before the storm comes,' he said quietly, 'I do not want you living under a leaking roof for weeks on end.'

There was no flicker of response.

He tried again. 'We've had plenty of warning about this flood. If we're not ready for it, there will be no second chance.'

Still nothing.

He looked past her. Their daughters-in-law were still there, ashen-faced. Noah understood that his project had reached a moment of utter crisis. He didn't know what to say.

'The boys wouldn't let me say "no" any longer.'

This comment brought a slight flicker of reaction. But he winced as he reflected on what he had said. It was terrible to blame his sons for what he had done.

Japheth joined the three young women. They were pointing at Jenaia's motionless form in front of them.

'It was weak of me,' Noah said, more strongly. 'I only dared do it because you were away.'

The faintest tilt in the angle of Jenaia's head informed him that he had found the right path.

'I should have asked you,' he continued. 'I could have asked you on any day in the past month.'

She still waited, her hands behind her back.

Noah now knew what he had to say.

It was not easy for him to say it. He paused, noting the mounting anxiety on the faces of the four silent watchers. And then he said, 'I'm sorry.'

He waited for a forgiving smile to spread across his dear wife's face.

None came.

He didn't know what to say now. Years of intense labour were teetering on the brink of calamity.

'I honestly believe that we cannot get this ark ready in time without the bronze tools,' he floundered. 'The flint-cut timbers let the rain in, and there is going to be a lot of rain, for a long time, and when we considered it all…' He faded into embarrassed silence.

Jenaia's expression had changed. She was giving him a familiar, 'Noah, I'm not stupid' look.

He pulled his lower lip between his teeth and bit it hard, looking directly into his wife's unfathomable eyes.

At last she spoke.

'Why us, Noah?'

'What?'

'Why us?'

'What do you mean?'

'Noah, think about it. You have lied to me. You have stolen from me. You have blamed your own children for your actions. And then there's me. I have put my own desires before my family's well-being. I have sworn at my sons for doing what they believed was right. Why us, Noah? Why does the Creator want to rescue us? We are no different from all the other stupid, selfish, squabbling people in this valley.'

Noah was taken aback. In all the years he had laboured without respite on this massive latticework of timber, he had never considered that question. And in all those years he had idly assumed that his wife would be cross with him for taking on such a mad project. He rarely mentioned his lifelong relationship with the Creator; it was a private matter. He was in no way prepared for such a conversation.

'You and I haven't killed any of our fellow humans,' he stated bluntly. That fact did indeed separate them from almost every other adult they knew – such were the days they were living in.

'I very nearly did today,' Jenaia announced quietly.

All this while her hands were behind her back. And Noah suddenly realised that her hands had been the focus of the young women's attention. Jenaia now brought her hands into view. She was holding a freshly sharpened bronze knife.

Noah looked at the new tool, and then into his wife's eyes. The blood rushed from his head, forcing him to lean against a wooden pillar to support himself. So she had climbed down to the lowest level of the ark to find her husband, fully intending to use it.

<hr />

It was a long, cold winter. When the roof was complete, the next task was to coat the entire structure, inside and out, with thick, black pitch. It was a daunting project. Noah's ark was one hundred and forty metres long, and over forty metres high. The pitch was purchased and transported by Shem, Ham and Japheth. Then it had to be softened over a fire and smeared over the timbers. The women had no choice but to abandon their homes and their friends in the village and pick up the pitch brushes. This was not a popular move. Shem's and Ham's wives, in particular, complained at every opportunity, and repeatedly had to be nagged into doing their share of the work. These were unhappy days for the whole family. The ark became their home. And as often as the four men huddled together to review the work, their wives assembled to air their complaints.

Through weeks of unprecedented snow, the fire inside the ark never went out. They worked in shifts, alternating between the unbearable heat of the fire for softening the pitch and the finger-numbing cold outside. During daylight hours, they worked on the outside of the ark. At night, they worked inside, in the dim glow of the fire. They ate meagre rations; they slept round the fire; they drank melted snow.

As the weeks passed they no longer argued. They had neither time nor energy for such frivolities. Just one leak in the ark's rough hull could cost them their lives. The job had to be done; it had to be done well; and it had to be done in time.

Noah constantly patrolled the three-dimensional maze of ladders and walkways, securing joints and panels, pointing out even the slightest patch of wood missed by the pitch brush. They hated him for it. But they also held him in unparalleled respect. The truth was that the only plan for this astounding ark lived in Noah's mind. Without Noah, they were all condemned to die in the coming flood.

They were too busy to notice the animals.

The villagers noticed them and were very afraid. There were regular sightings of wolves, leopards and bears in the vicinity of the ark, even mountain lions. The arrival of these creatures was taken as an omen of great evil. Whatever witchcraft was going on in that gargantuan black boat, the local people wanted nothing to do with it. Noah, they concluded, was cursed; and the wild animals circling his vast folly were a judgement from the gods. Up and down the valley, scattered communities made complex sacrifices to their deities, for protection. These were evil days. Noah, they believed, was doomed.

Noah and his family were unaware of all this. If they had a moment to notice that no one ever visited them or invited them to post-hunt revels, they would not have cared. They had a boat to finish. Always busy round a roaring fire, with pitch-stained clothes and filthy hands, they did not hear the unfamiliar songs of far-travelled birds, or the bark and howl of four-legged hunters.

Eventually the day came when the last section of their lifeboat's enormous hull was sealed with pitch. They had finished the outside weeks earlier. What remained were countless essential but inaccessible corners, where struts and buttresses of the interior framework met the hull. It was dissatisfying work.

For the third time, Noah sent the six younger people to survey every nook and cranny of their strange home, looking for patches of bare wood. This time, exhausted and grumpy, they failed to find one.

Noah, without much confidence, declared the ark complete. The family looked at one another with pale and weary faces, too tired to celebrate. They had not been outside for days. There had been no need. The ark was designed for self-sufficiency. The water tanks had been filled using barrowloads of snow (an unexpected blessing) and much of their stores were already aboard. They simply stared at each other, hardly daring to believe that they had achieved their aim. The ark was complete and the spring rains had not yet begun. They had no idea what time of day or night it was. Inside the black-coated ark it was always night and the air was thick with smoke and the stench of burning pitch.

They were on the lower deck, in the ark's only wide space, just inside the tall double doors. Shem said, 'Father, can we open the doors now?'

First they transferred the coals from their fire into the torch bowls mounted around the wide space. This was designed to be the family's main living area. Next, Noah insisted that they clear up the ash. 'There may be a wind,' he said. 'We don't want all of this blowing in our faces.' After that, the old man stood peering anxiously around in the torchlight. He could not think of another reason for not saying 'yes'.

Shem and Ham lifted and slid the heavy bolts that held the vast doors against the hull. Finally they pushed them open.

Spring rushed in: bright light, fresh air, familiar smells, a huge noise and hundreds of birds. Within seconds, a great cloud of assorted birds were pouring in through the open doorway. Noah and his family dived for cover at the invasion. They hid themselves in the narrow space under one of the ark's many ramps. After weeks of isolation, this assault was overpowering. The ark was suddenly filled with colour, movement and the music of a thousand twittering calls. Next came a scuttling sound and, within minutes, the newly cleared deck was carpeted with tiny creatures.

Noah watched, enraptured.

The Creator had instructed him to build an ark, so he had. Though he had been given the basic dimensions, he had to work out the detail of the structure himself. The project had consumed his every waking thought since that first day. It had never occurred to him to question where the animals would come from.

'I never imagined it would be like this,' Jenaia shouted over the racket of the arriving fauna. They both laughed. They had not done that in a long time.

Noah looked at his wife, squashed against him in their tight corner. He had learned a lot about her since the day she had decided not to kill him. He was not surprised to discover that she had been thinking long and hard about the matter of how they would find the animals.

But the animals had found them.

They were everywhere. There was not a patch of bare wood to be seen. Noah and his exhausted family watched in amazement. Creatures of which they had never dreamed ran around their feet, leapt onto rafters and beams, distributing themselves randomly around the vast boat. There were scuttlings and scratchings all around. As the pitch-laden smoke cleared, it was replaced by a new smell: the smell of life. Noah could do nothing but smile and wonder – suddenly aware of how much he had seriously doubted the threat of storm and flood. Now he knew for certain that the Creator meant everything he had said.

Time passed. There was no opportunity for Noah or his family to escape from their improvised sanctuary. Subtly, the noise on the outer ramp became louder and deeper. The stream of birds thinned, and the torrent of bugs and mini-beasts gave way to a flood of four-legged creatures. Hour by hour, these were becoming larger: wild cats, dogs, sheep, hyenas… all were now entering the ark.

What a spectacle!

'Look at that one,' someone would scream.

'And that!'

There was no noticeable pattern or order, apart from the fact that the animals were becoming gradually bigger. The ark's timbers were no longer coated with lines of tiny black shiny things; they had all disappeared into the tangle of timber and rope which held the ark together.

They were woken early by the sound of straining joints and creaking timbers. It was dark outside. Inside, torches glowed faintly, and the ark buzzed and creaked with nocturnal activity. Bats flitted in the doorway. A pair of lorises moved steadily along the rafter beside Noah's head. Outside, something was climbing the ramp, testing Noah's handiwork to its limit. Shem, Ham, Japheth and Noah looked at each other nervously. They understood what they were hearing. Their ramp was on the point of collapse, yet something was trying to get up it.

They stared out into the darkness. The floor between them and the doorway was now clear but for an aromatic coating of mud and dung. They listened as the beams and struts of the ramp tore apart. This creature, whatever it was, was bigger than they had imagined. And coming closer.

Japheth whispered to his wife, 'What's bigger than an elephant?'

Ham interjected, 'Have we got elephants? I've never seen one.'

'Two of them,' Japheth's wife told him.

'Where?'

'Over there. Look.'

There, indeed, was a pair of elephants, just like the ones very occasionally seen in their district, ridden by dark-faced eastern traders.

The ramp was breaking up.

It was uncertain which would happen first: the arrival of the monster or the destruction of the ramp. Seven of the cowering humans hoped it would be the ramp; Japheth's wife was the exception.

A dark shape blotted out their view of the distant treetops. There was a deafening crash. The creature let out a huge sound, the like of which they had never heard before, and there they were… two of them, filling the doorway… dark, vast and terrifying. These elephants weren't like the hump-backed ones from India. This pair was far larger. They dominated the family's open space as they stood with their tails, trunks and massive ears sweeping the night air.

By dawn the ark was still awash with activity. Squirrels and monkeys capered through the lifeless branches of the boat's muddled infrastructure. Noah blinked at the morning brightness. He was shocked to see a large number of creatures leaving down what was left of the ark's ramp. He panicked.

'Stop them!' he shouted, picking his way carefully across to the doorway.

The family gathered round him, wiping dung from their bare feet.

'We've only just got them all in,' Noah shouted over the constant noise of his once silent ark.

'They just need food,' Japheth's wife said steadily.

She was right.

For just a few moments, the previous day, they had allowed themselves to believe that their work was done. However, they still had more than half of the food stores to bring in from various barns and caves dotted around the construction site. It would be hard work bringing them up a broken ramp filled with creatures coming and going.

'WATCH IT!' someone shouted.

Two charging boars raced past them, scattering larger and smaller beasts in their wake.

'I need to listen to the Creator,' Noah said, as the family set to work. 'I need to find out what will happen next.'

IN THE DARK

Seven days.

That was all.

That was what the Creator had said. Seven days to transfer the remaining food stores aboard. There was no time to repair the ramp. It was easier to tether the elephants inside.

Noah gave the women the task of rounding up the animals that had escaped and keeping the rest on the ship. It proved impossible. No barricade could contain such a staggering range of escapologists. Eventually they gave up and concentrated their efforts on moving food. As Jenaia said, 'The animals made their way into the ark in the first instance. Surely they'll come back.'

Seven chaotic days. Animals were coming and going all day and all night. The humans were newly released from their winter confinement – and so were their tempers. It was seven days of shouting and blaming. By the end of the third day, the women and the men were sleeping at opposite ends of the ark. And with the darkening moods came darkening clouds. The wind turned. The temperature dropped.

Japheth and his wife had worked out a careful plan of which foodstuffs would be kept where. The plan had to be scrapped. The animals found their own niches – occupying many of the empty food store areas. Japheth shifted a huddle of mountain goats out of a fruit cupboard, and then watched as the goats attempted to turn a succession of other creatures out of their new homes.

Ultimately the goats returned to their cupboard, and the fruit was spilled, trampled and eaten.

'Noah,' Jenaia said purposefully. 'A few months ago, on the rare occasions when I ventured onto your ark, I could see no sense in the jumble of tree trunks and branches filling almost every available space. But you knew what each one of them was there for. I trusted you, Noah, and your ark holds together.'

'So far,' Noah muttered into his beard.

Jenaia returned to her bowl of porridge with a clear assumption that everything which needed to be said, had been said.

The rest of the family looked at her quizzically.

She took another mouthful.

Noah snapped. 'What has that to do with anything?'

Jenaia was reluctant to be distracted from her porridge. She couldn't remember when she had had such an appetite. Her only communication was a dismissive wave of her hand, which indicated, 'You work it out.'

Japheth got there first. He was most like his mother. 'Just because there doesn't seem to be any order to the animals' chaos,' he said reflectively, 'doesn't mean that there isn't any.'

He was rewarded by a grunt from his mother.

'So what do you recommend?' Noah was exasperated.

'Let the animals settle in their homes and then put the food wherever there's space,' Jenaia said. 'And try to put each type of food near the animals that eat it.'

'I have no idea what eats what!' Noah was still shouting.

'Then leave the animals to sort it out.' She slurped in another mouthful of porridge.

Noah stomped out. He hated to admit it, but she was right.

The rain began with a fine, misty drizzle, but quickly increased to a driving torrent, which brought the animals charging up the slippery ramp. Noah was in the middle of a frustrated attempt to count them. The large animals were easy enough to account for, but the smaller creatures rarely stayed still and often looked alike. He caught a glimpse of a field mouse scurrying along a rough beam, or was it two of them? How could he know? There were supposed to be two. But after a few seconds of trying to follow their – or its – progress, he gave up. God had asked for two of everything. As far as Noah could tell, there were at least two of most things. God would have to deal with the rest. Noah had the significant matter of shutting the doors to contend with.

Shem had made them practise closing the doors, several times over, before and after daubing them with pitch. It was obviously important to get it right.

But they had never tried shutting it in a storm-force wind with relentless rain, and the remnants of a shattered ramp getting in the way.

They struggled until it was dark on the evening of the eighth day. Then, soaked and exhausted, they gave up. The four men huddled together in one corner of the 'family space', which they now shared with four elephants, two giraffes and a pair of buffalo. The fire had been blown out by the gale, and all attempts to find a more sheltered, animal-free space to build another one had failed.

Everyone was tense.

Inside the ark there was incomprehensible muddle, unbearable noise and ceaseless activity. Outside there was a deadly storm. In their minds there was a nameless panic that they had not done quite enough; that even though they had built the ark, coated it in waterproof pitch, filled it with animals and transferred all the food stores, they would still die because they couldn't close the doors.

They watched as the doors swung freely, buffeted by the wind.

One of them slammed momentarily shut. Shem dived to grab it and tripped, sliding through a mixture of fresh dung, urine and rainwater before crashing into the leg of a sleeping elephant.

The opportunity was gone. The door swung open again.

Shem crawled through the slime, away from the startled elephant, and began to cry.

His wife joined him.

So did his mother.

And his brothers.

And their wives.

And finally Noah.

They had reached their limit. They had done so much. They had tried. They had worked, night and day, for months, for years. They had nothing left. They were at God's mercy.

At that moment, the storms within their souls were no less fierce than the one raging on the other side of the ark's black, sticky hull. They huddled together in numb despair, sharing whatever comfort they were able to afford each other.

They did not notice the air around them becoming still.

They were too wet to appreciate the absence of the rain.

It was God who closed the doors of Noah's ark, but the first the family knew of it was when the whole vessel suddenly lurched on its cradle, setting birds fluttering, large beasts howling, and sending the scamperers and the climbers careering here and there along every available log and branch that held the ark together.

The women shrieked.

The men swore.
The ark floated.

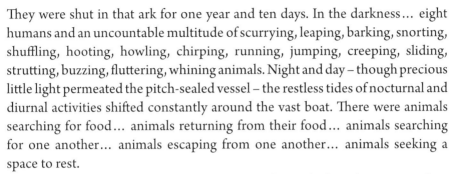

They were shut in that ark for one year and ten days. In the darkness... eight humans and an uncountable multitude of scurrying, leaping, barking, snorting, shuffling, hooting, howling, chirping, running, jumping, creeping, sliding, strutting, buzzing, fluttering, whining animals. Night and day – though precious little light permeated the pitch-sealed vessel – the restless tides of nocturnal and diurnal activities shifted constantly around the vast boat. There were animals searching for food... animals returning from their food... animals searching for one another... animals escaping from one another... animals seeking a space to rest.

For the first forty days, Noah's boat was driven before the most violent storm the earth had ever known. Then the rain stopped. But the wind did not. It continued to howl and whistle around the ark's rough timbers day after night, week after week. They pitched and rolled on the floodwaters for five whole months. For all those five months, the constant movement inside was matched by the equally constant movement of the ark on the waters. Noah and his family were no less a part of the constantly changing order within the ark. They would find a place to sleep and rest, and it would serve them well. Then one day they would find that a family of gazelles or a selection of geese, ducks and flamingos had taken a liking to their nook. Life on Noah's ark – the scavenging for food and drink as much as the search for space and bedding – was a free-for-all, and 'all' applied to everything on board, down to the last gnat.

There was a single window in the structure, right at the very top, which was kept firmly shut for fear of the inmates escaping. But, occasionally, one of the family would clamber the network of ladders and interlocking branches to take a quick peek at the world beyond. There was never anything to see but windswept seas.

Then, after five months afloat, they hit land. They hit it hard.

With a cacophony of crunching and scraping, they were dragged by tide and wind across a bed of hard rock. Every single creature on board was unsettled, floundering for equilibrium as the great ark jammed against an unknown mountain peak. While the humans hugged desperately onto the nearest sturdy branch, all but the largest animals hurtled around and around, causing the entire structure to lurch and tip.

Noah shouted to his sons to light torches and search the rancid depths of the ark for damage to the hull. For hours, all eight of them laboured with saw and mallet and pitch to stop the leaks. Mercifully, there was no major breach.

Gradually, life aboard settled back to the more usual level of chaos. Hopes rose – temporarily – that their ordeal might be over. But it was to be another ten weeks before the first peaks of the mountain tops were spotted from the window. And, with the ark itself now motionless, the animals were more active than ever. Some of the larger creatures finally dared to climb and roam – the lions, wild dogs and deer among them.

How it was for the humans aboard remains best untold. Let it suffice to say that humans too are animals and just as susceptible to squabbles over territory or competition for the best food, or challenges for supremacy. The detail of what took place among Noah's family in that dark boat on those dark days is known only to God. And God is discreet.

But they did celebrate Noah's birthday. It was a big one: a number with two zeros at the end. By then they had been cooped up in the darkness for nearly ten months, even though the rains had long since ended. With Noah's permission – for he had indeed maintained his supremacy – Shem, Ham and Japheth began to cut away the outer covering of the ark's roof, allowing the light of the sun to penetrate the intricate latticework of fine branches into which the thatch had been woven.

For the first time, by the light of the sun, Noah and his family saw just how many creatures there were crammed into their ark. Even though they had heard them day and night, even though they had pushed past them each time they needed to clamber their way from one place to another, they were astounded when the sunlight revealed what they had only ever felt and fumbled at.

Owing to the limitations of the flint axes, Noah had constructed the interior framework of the ark from a jumbled mass of small trunks and branches, all lashed together in a random pattern using lengths of reed.

'This one's a bit wobbly,' he had announced in those long-forgotten days of fresh air, fresh food and fresh water. 'Shem, Ham, run a supporting strut from here to there, and fix it firmly to that one as it passes.'

And so the vast inner expanse of his ark was like the tangle of a forest canopy, enclosed on all sides, without the space that tree trunks provide between branch and forest floor, and without the subtle order that is the hallmark of the Creator's work. Every single one of these unnumbered timbers had become a home. And as the first light flooded inside, small, blinking circles of reflected light could be seen in all directions, as far as the light reached.

It was a day of great celebration for the family. For the other creatures, however, the invading light caused enormous upheaval. The bats that had up to then slept peacefully in the roof timbers, fled to the lowest depths, followed by all the other night-loving beasts. At the same time, the light-lovers, from parakeets to cheetahs, sped lightwards. The mayhem lasted several days as every creature, apart from a few contented woodworms, was obliged to seek new lodgings in the newly divided world of light and darkness.

The great southern elephants, of course, were also unmoved. There was nowhere else for them to go.

In many ways, the last two months were the hardest. Through the entwined cage that was their roof, the family could see newly exposed land in all directions. But Noah would not allow them to open the doors.

'It is not enough for the flood to have receded,' he argued (and this matter was constantly argued). 'We have to wait until there is enough food out there for everyone in here.'

'But do we have enough food on the ark?' Ham argued in return.

'It won't be long before the animals start eating one another,' Japheth's wife added gloomily.

'When that day comes,' Noah reassured them, 'we will certainly open the doors. But for now we wait.'

'Wait for what?' The question had been posed a hundred times, in every mood and tone of voice known to humankind, most often by Shem's young and once beautiful wife.

Noah gave his familiar answer. That is, he didn't answer.

Though no one said it, everyone knew. He was waiting for directions from the Creator.

None came.

There did come a day when Noah impatiently released a raven through the precious window, to see what it would do. It swooped and glided on the currents of the air, round and round in ever-increasing circles until they could see it no more. This only multiplied their impatience. It did not answer any of their questions.

A week later, Noah let free a different species of bird – a dove. They watched it all day. It flitted around restlessly. Come evening, Noah stretched his arm out through the window and brought the exhausted bird back inside.

It was a quiet evening in the humans' huddle. No one argued. They all knew that they would have to wait. They waited impatiently. Shem's wife lobbied her husband to push Noah for specific assurances but none came.

A week later, after much nagging, Noah sent the same dove out again. The whole family perched among the roof timbers, straining to follow its progress. To a mixture of excitement and disappointment, the creature flew out of view, down the side of the mountain, which they had identified as the mountain called Ararat.

Shem's wife organised a watch. One member of the family was to sit up there all day, looking for the dove.

Jenaia was the last to take her turn. Jammed precariously between forked branches not far from the window, she watched the orange sun make its dignified descent behind the distant sea.

'It's back, it's back,' she screamed as the dove fluttered a few feet above her grey head. The younger members of the family were quick to shin their way up now familiar pathways, careless of the creatures that were obliged to make way for them. Noah went to his window and reached out an arm. In the dove came, and in its beak it brought a freshly plucked olive leaf – a single leaf.

Never in human history has one leaf brought so much joy! They sat round their small fire – they had recently begun to burn parts of the ark itself, so scant were their resources – and they passed the leaf around, again and again, each wondering at its freshness and softness.

'So, do we leave tomorrow?' Ham asked, prompted by Shem's wife.

Noah said nothing. He sat motionless, eyes closed.

He made them wait another week. It was a bad-tempered week. It was particularly bad-tempered on the third day when someone dropped the prized olive leaf and it was eaten by a passing something. Noah was nagged continually by the rest of the family to release the dove again. It was never quite clear which they wanted more: to get off the ark or to get a replacement leaf. But subtly, as the week progressed, the mood changed. There was a new tension in the air, unspoken, unspecified, but very real.

After seven days, Noah released the dove for a third time. This time they watched it with ambivalence. When not on watch – and no one was in a hurry to watch – the four couples kept to themselves. The animals were as noisy as ever, but the humans were quiet.

The sun set, darkness came, and the dove didn't return.

The family sat around their fire in uncomfortable silence.

Jenaia and Noah looked at one another with an understanding known only to those who have devotedly loved one another for many, many years.

Jenaia spoke.

'I didn't want us to stop farming in order to build this silly boat,' she said. 'I thought it was the end of the world.' There was a long pause during which they all gazed into the randomness of the flames. 'I didn't want to leave my home to live in this mess and muddle,' she continued. 'But I had to.' Another long pause. 'I didn't want the rain to start, but it did. I didn't want the animals to take over our ark, but they came.'

Her pause at this stage was very long indeed. It was so long that they all assumed her to have finished and each one struggled to catch the wisdom they didn't doubt was there.

One by one, they were distracted from their ponderings as they noticed the tears running down Jenaia's wrinkled cheeks. She began to sob loudly. Japheth's wife put an arm around her.

Eventually, Jenaia completed her story. 'Now,' she sniffed, 'now I am afraid to leave.' She looked across the circle, with tear-filled eyes, to Noah. 'I have come to… ' She never finished. Her feelings flooded out and caught up the rest of her family in their flow.

That night, exhausted by their emotions, they slept together around the fire on the highest deck of Noah's ark.

They were woken most strangely… by rain dripping from the open roof above them. It was not a storm, but the light refreshing rain of a warm, bright morning. Shem's wife screamed. Ham swore. All three younger couples leapt into action, desperate to do something to stop their year-long ordeal from starting all over again. Shem and Ham vainly tried to re-cover the open roof. Japheth and his wife fetched containers to catch the rain. They shouted aimlessly at one another, and at their unseen Creator too. And throughout this drama, Noah lay on his back, face to the falling rain, smiling.

The children were far too flustered to notice the old man's mood. It was not until he laughed out loud that he gained their attention. The six of them stared in utter bemusement at the old man's shining, rain-soaked face.

Noah laughter became a childlike giggle. The more he was aware of them waiting for him, the harder he found it to control. His recovery was not helped by Jenaia, who joined him in his helpless amusement. The two of them were soon doubled up and rolling helplessly on the damp floor. It took a furiously demanding, 'WHAT?' from Ham, who had climbed down from the roof, to shake Noah out of it.

'If you want to build a shelter,' the patriarch spluttered through barely controlled laughter, do it out there.' He pointed towards the mountain plain on which the ark was jammed, and began chortling again.

Ham was not amused. 'You won't let us out.'

When he had recovered enough composure, Noah replied, 'You can go now, now that it's raining.'

'You're crazy,' Ham bawled, well aware of the seriousness of his accusation.

'I know,' Noah giggled. 'It's the rain.'

The family stared at him, waiting for an explanation. By now they were all soaked. The sight of the six furious, rain-drenched people was suddenly sobering, reminding Noah of the many thousands who had lost their lives in the Creator's flood.

'You have to learn to trust,' he told his bewildered family.

Only Jenaia showed any sign of understanding.

Noah added. 'If the land is ready for more rain, it is ready for us.'

He pulled his ancient bones upwards and hobbled down the slippery ramps that led to the ark's great doors. He paused to stroke affectionately a number of animals on his way. There was a serene sadness in his eyes.

Shem, Ham and Japheth were on hand to open the doors. But they could not budge them.

While his sons fought the sea-swollen timbers, Noah looked around him at the staggering mass of animalkind which had crowded into his ark. It would be comforting to think that the animals observed the significance of this moment with a dignified silence. They did not. They were hurtling, wandering, and clomping around the familiar pathways just as much as they ever had.

'Stand clear,' Japheth's wife shouted from somewhere up high.

She had climbed onto the neck of one of the elephants and was urging the creature forwards by crashing her bare heels against its shoulders. It worked. The massive pachyderm lumbered towards the door and did not stop. Light cascaded in. Animals cascaded out, led by the elephant picking its way down a ramp of rubble which the ark had piled up invisibly on the day it ground to a halt on Mount Ararat. The humans were swept along by the animal tide.

Only then did they realise just how subdued the animals had actually been through their long incarceration... because now they were going completely berserk. And the noise was phenomenal.

Noah clambered up onto an island of rock in the flood of flesh. From his vantage point, he searched intently. One by one his family joined him. Still the animals belched out of the redundant ark. The rain continued, light and fresh.

'What are you looking for?'

It was an obvious question.

'A sign.' The answer was passed on to each new arrival on the rocky outcrop.

'A sign... of what?'

'Dad hasn't said.'

The sun came out.

Ham's wife let out an awestruck, 'Oh, wow!'

The others blinked into the brightness of the sun. It was wonderful to see it unimpeded by the ark's latticework roof. But was it that impressive?

Ham's wife seemed to think so. 'What the . . .?'

Ham looked behind to see why his wife was so taken by the emerging sun, and let out an overwhelmed, 'Oooooh!'

The rest of the family turned too.

Across the light grey sky was stretched a curved ribbon of bright, coloured lights: violet, indigo, blue, green, yellow, orange and soft red, all blending into one another. They had never seen anything like it.

Noah spoke very quietly. 'That is what I was looking for.'

ORDER FROM CHAOS

R ACHAEL LAY AWAKE, listening. She was listening for anything… to everything… for something that would give a hint of an answer to her nightly question: What was Boaz up to?

It was an old routine. Back in Egypt, during their years of forced labour, Boaz's night-time activities were necessary. Under the cover of darkness, he would slip out of the Israelite compound and ghost his way around the homes of wealthy Egyptians, searching for discarded food. It was a matter of survival. There was never enough food in the labour camps, nor time to produce it. Every day there were bricks to be made, targets to be met… impossible targets. And when the labourers fell short of those targets, they were beaten and their food rations were cut. Boaz didn't only gather food for his own family. Many others benefited from his nightly expeditions.

Rachael and Boaz had never known any other life. Boaz had been taught the art of stealth by his father. He, in turn, had trained his own sons. He saw it as simple justice. The Egyptians had more than they needed. They had it because they could have it, because they controlled the markets and made the laws. With their wealth they strengthened their grip on everyone else's lives.

Boaz's father had been forced off his family's land and sent to the labour compound to make bricks. Boaz had been born there, so had his children. Five of the seven children born to Boaz and Rachael had been taken from them, to be slaves in ornate Egyptian villas, and not all of them had escaped back to the family when Moses led them to freedom. Life had been so hard. But now, that was all over.

Rachael listened to the silence of the night. It was so different. Away from the stifling heat of the Nile valley, she had still to adapt to the cool night air of the mountains. Gone was the familiar noise of Egyptian parties; there was only the muted conversation of tired people crowded into small travelling tents. It would have been wonderful simply to lie there and soak in the sound of freedom, if only Boaz and Enan were with her in the tent.

She knew her husband and son were not searching for food. Now they had all the food they could eat, every day. Nor for clothes: the family's clothing was in excellent condition. Yet, more often than not, when he thought that Rachael was asleep, Boaz would slip out quietly into the darkness. Sometimes he would take young Enan with him.

Rachael had tried asking Boaz about it, but his replies were always evasive and Enan was unswervingly loyal to his dad. She often considered following them, but she never did. She had their youngest, little Sarai, to look after, and she lacked her husband's expertise in the ways of the night. Also, something in her mind told her that it was not for her to go creeping after Boaz; it was up to him to trust her with the truth.

So she lay awake and wondered and worried and waited.

In the morning, when Rachael woke, Boaz was asleep beside her. She took Sarai outside and the two of them gathered enough food for the family: six measures of the strange desert food for which they still had no name. They simply called it 'what is it?' because that's what everyone said when they first encountered the nutritious white grain-like substance which carpeted the Israelite encampment each morning. Mother and daughter then ground the grains into flour, and kneaded and baked it into round, flat breads. The men were woken by the smell of breakfast.

'We're packing up today,' Boaz announced. 'I heard it last night. Moses is taking us further up into the mountains, to where he used to live.'

This had been the pattern of their lives for weeks: meandering across the bald desert, looking for enough sparse vegetation to feed the livestock, setting up camp, staying a few days, then moving on. They all knew what was expected of them, but that didn't prevent these from being the most stressful of days. Rachael was in charge – shouting, nagging, threatening. Enan was dispatched, eventually, to relieve one of his older brothers from minding their few goats. Boaz dismantled the tent. Rachael did everything else, with a little bit of help, when it suited them, from the other members of the family. And Boaz's elderly mother sat and watched, and muttered under her breath.

'Where's the big leather bag?' Rachael yelled above the hubbub of an entire community preparing to move on.

'It was behind the tent, underneath all the others,' Boaz replied.

'Well, it's not there now.'

'It was there yesterday.'

'WELL, IT'S NOT THERE NOW.'

'Let me have a look.'

'Boaz, I'm not stupid. I can tell whether a large leather bag is there or not.'
Nonetheless, he looked.

'Hmmm…'

'Now do you believe me?'

'It was there last night.'

'You already said.'

'I'll get you another one tonight.'

He returned to his task, leaving Rachael to ponder, yet again, the nature of his nocturnal wanderings; also leaving her to decide what to leave behind – because they would not be able to carry so much without the bag.

She swore, cursing the God of her Israelite ancestors. Why was life so unfair? Back in Egypt things regularly went missing. She always blamed the Egyptians. Now the Egyptians were a desert away. So she blamed God.

After that, no member of the family was able to do anything right in Rachael's eyes. Boaz kept to himself; Abdon, one of her older sons, shouted as much as he was shouted at; her mother-in-law rested in preparation for another day of walking, while also looking after Sarai. Only Enan was safe, beyond the perimeter of the camp, surrounded by goats.

Then, just when all was nearly ready, a stranger, an attractive young woman, walked up to Rachael and handed over an empty leather bag.

'Boaz told me your bag's been stolen,' she said. 'Here, you can borrow this.'

Rachael turned around to give her husband a questioning look. He was nowhere to be seen. After she had scoured the immediate neighbourhood with her gaze, she turned back to the girl, only to discover that she had gone too, part skipping and part running her way through the forest of half-dismantled tents and waiting travellers.

Rachael pushed away the questions inside her head. She would have to repack, and some families were already leaving.

There was no time to think. Travelling days were like that… shuffling the different loads between friends and family, keeping track of excited children, dealing with a moaning mother-in-law. Rachael was glad of the extra bag, though she still had to leave some things behind. Mostly, she left Boaz's possessions, because she was cross with him. If she'd had time, she would have considered whether or not she felt guilty for doing so. But there were too many other concerns pressing for her attention.

At the end of a day of walking, climbing higher into the mountains, in cooler air, on rougher ground, after the tent was pitched and the day's bread consumed, Rachael slept the sleep of an exhausted mother. When she woke, Boaz was not there. His bed covers were still folded where she had placed them the night before. After gathering food for the day and baking it, she noted that the borrowed leather bag was also missing. In the fragments of time between countless interruptions, Rachael attempted to piece together these clues. She made little progress.

'What's the matter with you?' Boaz's mother asked sharply.

Rachael didn't feel able to explain. Even if she understood the situation herself, she was not sure it would be wise to tell the old woman. She pulled a face in reply.

'You should go and see Moses about it,' her mother-in-law suggested.

That's what everyone did. Every time there was an argument, people went to Moses. But Rachael never did. She didn't consider her problems important enough to bother the great man. What were a few domestic tensions in comparison with the demands of twelve interrelated tribes of liberated slaves?

Boaz's mother would not drop the subject. She had a mother's art for nagging. By late morning, Rachael resolved that she would take her problem to Moses, simply in order to get away from the constant flow of stories about different people whose problems were resolved by the old man.

As she made her way to the centre of the encampment, she tried to assemble her thoughts, to work out precisely what her problem was. She didn't want to embarrass herself in front of the man who had taken on the pharaoh of Egypt and won.

She needn't have bothered. There was such a crowd of people waiting for Moses' attention that Rachael never made it to the front of the queue. As the light of the stars began to pierce the evening sky and the temperature plummeted, Rachael picked her way back towards her tent, in search of food and a warm blanket.

Boaz was already in bed.

'Where's my statue?' he grouched when he heard his wife arrive.

'What statue?' She knew perfectly well. It was a carved figure of a naked woman with a wolf's head that Boaz had 'liberated' from an Egyptian home when he was a young man. It was some Egyptian goddess, and he had always been rather proud of it. Rachael had abandoned it with the rubbish at their previous camp.

At that moment she found an answer to one of her unanswered questions from the past two days. She did not feel guilty for leaving it. She was glad that the ghastly thing was gone. She was relieved to be free of the oppressive gaze of Egyptian religion. She looked up at the brightening stars and thanked their Creator that, for all her present problems, she was no longer a slave in Egypt.

Early the next morning, Rachael shoved Boaz awake. 'You'll have to gather the food today,' she told him. 'I need to speak to Moses.'

'He won't have time for you, you stupid woman! Anyway, I don't know how to cook the stuff.'

'Just boil it in water. I don't care.'

She left.

A short distance from her tent, Rachael spotted the young woman who had loaned her the leather bag. She was not sure whether to scowl or smile.

She smiled.

Her early start paid off. There were only a few others waiting outside Moses' tent; all of them people she recognised from the day before. Moses was not there. She sat down and gazed up at the rocky mountain looming over the camp. When she saw Moses, his wife, and their two boys returning from gathering food together – as a family – Rachael was jealous.

When her turn came, she sat in her leader's unremarkable tent and fumbled her way through the mysteries of Boaz's nocturnal habits, unknown young women and disappearing bags.

Moses – former shepherd, ex-member of the Egyptian royal family and son of brick-making Israelite slaves – listened patiently. When the tale was over, he sighed an exhausted sigh.

Rachael's emotions broke free. 'I don't know what's right and what isn't,' she sobbed, catching her tears in her tunic.

'No one does,' Moses reflected. 'That's why we have come to this mountain.'

Rachael failed to understand. What difference would a mountain make?

'When I've been up the mountain,' Moses informed her, 'I may be able to help you.'

'When are you going?' It still didn't make sense to her but it was the only hope she had.

'Soon.'

Later that day, as happened so often, Boaz was the one who knew what was happening.

'He's left us,' he announced indifferently, sipping the soupy broth he had made for the family that morning.

'Who has?'

'Moses. He's gone up the mountain.'

Rachael's heart raced, but she maintained a veneer of calm disinterest.

Boaz continued, 'It's why he brought us here, apparently.' He half turned to look at the craggy mountain behind him. 'It was somewhere up there that he met God and was told to rescue us all from Egypt. Now – job done – he's gone up to report back … or something.'

Rachael looked longingly into the shadowy distance. Somewhere up there, she hoped, was the resolution of all the things that did not add up in her life. Up there was the key to being a 'normal' family, like Moses and Zipporah were.

She went to bed alone and was woken by Boaz, his eyes shining. He and Enan had already been out and collected the family's daily supply of food.

'Moses is back,' he told her. 'He's called a general assembly at midday.'

Rachael could hear the buzz of anticipation around the camp.

The family went together. All except for Enan, who was on goatherd duty. The area around Moses' tent was densely packed with clumps of people seated wherever there was enough space between the muddled tents. Moses himself was working his way round the vast crowd. But rumour travelled faster than the venerable leader. He was speaking to every family, every clan. He had struck an arrangement with God and was explaining the conditions attached.

It was a long wait. Sarai was bored. Mother-in-law was uncomfortable. Boaz was restless, always looking around, studying the crowd. Rachael was both full of hope and racked with anxiety.

Eventually Moses picked his way into the middle of their group.

'I have spoken with God,' he announced, 'the God of our ancestors Abraham, Isaac and Israel. He has rescued you from Egypt, and chosen you to be his own people. If you live his way, you will always be his treasured nation.'

'So what do we have to do?'

Rachael was embarrassed to hear Boaz being so bold in such a public setting.

Moses' reply was well practised; he had given it many times that day: 'Don't serve, or worship any other gods, be content with the property and family that you have, and always be honest to God and one another.'

Rachael watched Boaz carefully. He was blushing, and looking away into the distance. But within herself she felt relief. She still didn't quite understand it, but somehow those simple instructions gave her the beginnings of the framework she longed for.

'So will you do it?' Moses called out confidently. 'Will you be God's people?'

'We will!'

'Yes!'

'Of course!'

The people's replies were laden with optimism.

Rachael shouted, 'Thank you!'

Boaz continued to stare into the distance.

That night, Boaz's bed remained empty, but once again he gathered the family's food – this time alone. Moses, he reported, had gone back up the mountain and there would be another assembly in the afternoon.

Come the afternoon, Boaz offered to watch the goats so that Enan could join the assembly.

Rachael overruled.

Once again, Moses insisted on delivering God's message in person. He did not trust rumour and gossip. 'God is going to speak to you all,' he explained. 'He is going to unfold the way you are to live, to be his treasured people. Now, go back to your tents. Wash yourselves. Wash your clothes. And keep yourselves pure – today and tomorrow. On the third day, God will show himself to you on this mountain.'

There was urgency in Moses' voice. These strange instructions mattered. 'You must wait at the bottom of the mountain,' he insisted. 'You must not go up until you hear the ram's horn sound. Then you may go up and meet your God, the Creator of the stars.'

It was serious business. No one doubted that. Never before had a god – any god – appeared to an entire nation. The gods of Egypt occasionally popped up in legends, but never like this. People were nervous. Boaz was very quiet and Rachael kept him within sight every moment of those two days. She even threaded the doorway of their tent together at night, tying both ends of the thread round her own ankle. She was taking no risks; the future of her family depended on it.

On the morning of the third day they were all woken by the sound of approaching thunder. Distant rumbles quickly became sharp crashes. The family lay in their tent and waited for the sound of rain.

None came.

Rachael unthreaded the tent's opening and looked outside. Mount Sinai was smothered in smoke. The rocky, barren mountain appeared to be on fire, though there was little on it that would burn. One by one, her family joined her and stared in terror at the trembling mountain. This God was no perfect-breasted woman with an animal's head.

No one said much. No one ate much. They dressed in clean clothes and walked silently to the foot of the mountain. Moses had appointed armed stewards to mark out a boundary around the mountain and to remind people that they must not – on pain of death – venture up the mountain until they were instructed to do so. There was little fear of that. The once innocuous peak had become a living, blazing terror. No one in their right mind would go up there.

Except Moses.

There was an audible gasp when people saw the familiar form of their leader striding purposefully towards them out of the fire and smoke. He stepped through the line of stewards – each holding a loaded bow – and reminded the Israelites to remain where they were.

They did.

Then God spoke.

No two people quite had the same memory of that moment. Those that did actually hear something with their ears remembered different sounds. Some recalled trumpets, others peals of thunder. Many, Rachael among them, experienced the event as simply 'knowing'... knowing things they had not known before. Whatever their descriptions of the encounter with their Creator, every person without exception heard (or remembered) ten distinct messages. And in every person's mind, those messages were the same:

You must not worship any other gods.

You must not worship any handmade figure in any shape.

You must not abuse God's name.

Work for no more than six days, then rest.

Respect your mother and father. If you do, I will look after you.

Do not murder.

Do not commit adultery.

Do not steal.

Do not lie.

Do not be jealous of your neighbour's family, or their possessions.

Those were the words that they all received. There was no doubt, no disagreement. To Rachael, God's words came like soothing ointment on a festering wound; like beautiful music after a night of angry shouting. She stood, eyes closed, breathing in the glorious simplicity of these instructions. Moses had been right when she had visited him in his tent: he had been up the mountain and it had helped her.

For Boaz, the words of God were like ten slaps across the face. It was as though he had looked into a mirror for the first time in his life and seen just how ugly he was. He kept asking different people what they had heard, always hoping that someone would have a more sympathetic interpretation. But each time God's commandments only slapped him a further ten times.

There was much talk among the Israelites. People's minds were saturated. Gradually, the hubbub distilled itself into messages that were passed up to the heads of the families. One by one, an assortment of tribal representatives sought out Moses. Their messages were the same: 'The people can't take any more of this. You go up the mountain alone to meet God. We will wait for you down here.'

The people – or, more accurately, most of the people – were scared by all they had heard and seen. Moses tried to reassure the representatives, but their demand did not change.

After a period of negotiation, it was agreed that Moses would go up the fire-covered mountain again. He would take with him the seventy representatives, also his brother Aaron and his young assistant Joshua. Rachael watched in rapt amazement as the representatives embraced their families with anxious farewells and assembled around Moses. Then they climbed their way slowly up the narrow mountain path and disappeared into the cloud of smoke.

No one moved for a long time.

Gradually, people began to relax. Children started playing. Groups of women began to talk, and men turned their attention to other matters. There was a limit to how long the trauma of the mountain could hold their attention; they sought refuge in the minor details of life.

Rachael continued to look up into the smoke and fire for a long time. She was trying to imagine what Moses and the others might be doing. Part of her was jealous; another part relieved. Boaz sat beside her, his head buried in his hands. He did not speak again that day.

The cooling sun swelled and reddened towards the western horizon and people began to drift back to their tents. Children needed supper and their beds. There were jobs to be done. Rachael sent her family home. She resolved to wait for Moses' return.

As the fading sun dipped its lower edge into the distant and unseen Nile, the group of tribal representatives emerged into view where the mountain track met the opaque smoke of God's presence. Rachael stood and advanced to the line of armed stewards, all still at their posts. She peered through the gathering gloom, searching for Moses among the small crowd.

A few others with her, also waiting, murmured, 'Can you see him?'

'I think that's him, near the back.'

'You mean the one in the red cloak?'

'Yes.'

'No, that's Nadab, I'm fairly sure.'

Slowly they drew to the conclusion that Moses was not there. As the group came closer, names were identified, heads were counted. There were two people missing: young Joshua and Moses. The remaining seventy-one looked… well, no one quite managed to put it into words. They looked invigorated, yet also tired; inspired, somehow awestruck.

They were greeted by a barrage of questions and struggled to answer them. The general content of their report was that Moses had been called further up the mountain, and that Joshua was waiting for him. The rest of them had been told to return and get on with their lives.

One piece of information stood out for Rachael. Aaron kept repeating it: 'God has promised to give Moses some stone tablets, inscribed with the commands that he spoke this morning.' This thrilled her. She was so tired of uncertainty. To have God's simple instructions written in stone, for all generations, was a wonderful prospect. If they were written in stone there would be no more uncertainty. Boaz would have to live within their boundaries.

Her heart swelling with hope, she returned to her tent, taking her husband by the hand as she went. He did not abandon his silence, but she squeezed his hand in reassurance as they walked together.

Everything was going to be all right.

The following days were busy with all the usual things. Goats had to be milked, food had to be gathered, bread had to be baked, cheese had to be made, children had to be cared for, as did mothers-in-law and husbands. On the sixth day, as had been the pattern for some weeks, they gathered enough food for two days. On the seventh day, in accordance with the fourth of God's instructions, Rachael insisted that her family rested. She hid Boaz's tool bag, and his mother's sewing kit. She insisted that no one worked. When Boaz argued that, at the very least, someone had to watch the goats and milk the poor creatures, Rachael declared that the whole family would watch the goats together, and that they would drink the milk straight away.

In the end, Grandma was permitted to stay in the tent and sleep. The rest of them wandered together round the foothills of Sinai, followed by their bleating goats. By the afternoon even Boaz was showing signs of enjoying himself as he joined his children in a game of hide-and-seek. They chattered together over a supper of bread and fresh milk on the edge of the sprawling camp. And Rachael looked up at the mysterious mountain and thanked God for his fourth commandment.

Another week passed. Moses still did not return. The mood in the camp slowly reverted to its former ways. Distressing rumours circulated, squabbles were rekindled, blood was spilt. And Boaz resumed his night-time wanderings. Rachael's hope faded. Soon it felt as though nothing had changed – only that Moses was no longer available to patch up the Israelites' problems. Aaron tried to fill the vacancy, but he lacked his younger brother's strength of mind.

Whenever she had the opportunity, Rachael still made her way to the foot of the smoke-covered mountain to stand and wonder for a while about God, Moses and the promised rules carved into stone. As the days succeeded one another, fewer and fewer people did the same. Becoming familiar with the fire and smoke of the mountain, they ignored it more and more. Their conversation returned to the gods of the Egyptians – gods people could touch and see and understand. They wanted that kind of a god for themselves.

More than a month passed and neither Moses nor Joshua had returned. Boaz informed his family that Aaron was collecting gold.

'Why?' Rachael asked.

'To make a god,' Boaz explained, 'like other nations have.'

'Well, he's not having any of mine,' said Rachael defiantly.

'You have to give your earrings,' Boaz explained.

Rachael swiftly removed the thick Egyptian hoops from her ear lobes and held them tightly in her fist. 'I don't have any!'

'He can have mine, dear,' Grandma said, passing them to Boaz.

The whole family looked at young Sarai, who looked anxiously back at them. Rachael blinked and sighed. She knew she was outnumbered. Still holding her own earrings, she crawled out of the tent and walked to the foot of the mountain. There she could be alone – alone with her fading hope that there might be an end to the exhausting muddle in her family's life.

She stared desperately into the swirling grey smoke, hoping against hope to catch a glimpse of Moses and the stone tablets, inscribed with God's liberating words. Several times she fancied that she had spotted his long hair and thick beard, but it was only ever an illusion, like the tormenting mirages on the desert floor.

Aaron announced a general assembly for midday the next day. He had conceded to the people's demands; he had fashioned the Israelites' pooled gold into a god – their own god. This was, so the rumours went, quite different from the stylised deities of Egypt. It was a unique god for a unique people; a rugged symbol for a nation who made their living in the rocky mountain pastures of Sinai.

All morning the camp was buzzing with anticipation of its first encounter with this new god. Boaz was full of intriguing hints. He was clearly involved in the plans for this occasion and told everyone who passed, 'Take plenty of food. Slaughter the fattest animal in your flock. If you have been saving any wine, tonight's the night!' He insisted that his family set off early for the assembly, so they could be at the front. The sense of excitement grew.

Many tents in the centre of the camp had been cleared away, including Moses' own. There was no sign of his wife and children. Precisely where Moses' tent had been, there stood a carved rock plinth. Whatever was set on top of the plinth – presumably the new god – was covered with a linen shroud. Rachael looked at it uneasily.

Boaz engaged those around him in an extended guessing game about what form this god might display. As the sense of anticipation rose, his guessing game became a betting game. Enan was recruited to record the bets received – pieces of gold, silver jewellery, polished stones, promises of cheeses.

Rachael said accusingly to her husband, 'You know what it is, don't you?'

He defended his actions. 'I have not forced anyone to take part.'

She turned her back on him.

As the sun reached its highest point, Aaron and a few of the tribal leaders processed their way through the crowd and assembled around the covered plinth. They were dressed in crude mock-ups of the robes worn by the high priests of Egypt. This brought a resounding cheer from the people. This was something familiar, something they understood, something more accessible than the forbidden mountain.

There were incantations in the Egyptian style. A fire was lit on a small stone altar beside the plinth. Frankincense was thrown into its flames, causing billows of pungent smoke.

Rachael watched impassively. Boaz was bolt upright with anticipation, still receiving bets as they were passed through the crowd towards him.

A glossy-coated bull was dragged forwards, causing a fresh wave of punters to join Boaz's game. While Enan struggled to keep up with the book keeping, Boaz stood and indicated that his book was now closed; no more bets would be accepted.

The bull was grabbed by its horns and wrestled to the ground. Aaron stood by while Nadab took a long knife and sliced the creature's throat, collecting its gushing blood in a clay bowl. The people rose, raised their arms and cheered, sending a wave of movement back to the distant edge of the assembly.

Aaron stepped forward and indicated to everyone to sit.

'Children of Abraham,' he shouted, 'children of Isaac and Israel, listen to me.'

They did. But it was not a moment for long speeches. With so many thousands of people, the message had to be conveyed in relays to the back of the crowd. Aaron spoke in tightly clipped phrases, and the people – eager to see what their god really looked like – were quiet.

'People of Israel…'

Self-appointed heralds, just managing to pick out Aaron's words, stood and broadcast them to those seated further away from the shrouded idol.

'Your God rescued you from Egypt…'

The message was passed on.

'Your God feeds you with desert bread…'

This was met with a murmur of appreciation.

Sensing that the people's patience was limited, Aaron took hold of the fringe of the linen shroud which covered his handiwork. Almost all the eyes of a nation were trained on Aaron, apart from a few who were looking hopefully towards Boaz. Boaz felt the strain of the moment. Certainty is a brittle substance. Even though he had already seen beneath the linen shroud, he was now subject to sharp pangs of fear and doubt.

Aaron pulled at the shroud. The self-appointed priests declared together, 'THIS IS YOUR GOD!'

Israel roared to its feet in deafening unison – apart from Boaz, who hugged his bagful of precious metal and semi-precious stones.

Rachael felt sick.

Fixed to the top of the plinth, at a careless angle, was a childish representation of a calf. Aaron, evidently, was no craftsman.

As the nation's cheering died away, Nadab proclaimed: 'Let the festival begin.'

Musicians began to play frantic music. Skins of Egyptian wine were produced and cut open.

In the confusion, Rachael picked her way past reddening faces and coarse laughter to the edge of the camp, to the foot of Moses' mountain. She was not, at that moment, remembering the second of God's great commands. She was moved by a deep sadness that Moses, their rescuer and their guide, had so quickly been forgotten.

She was not the only one to leave the party. Already there, huddled pathetically together, were Moses' wife Zipporah and their two sons. Rachael did not presume to join them. She stood, aloof and alone, staring up hopelessly into the fire-drenched mountain.

She did not return to her tent that night. Nor did most of the Israelites. The sound of dancing and drunken laughter continued through dawn, past noon and on into the following evening. Rachael did not sleep. She huddled under her woollen cloak and tried not to imagine what Boaz might be doing.

She failed.

Repeatedly, she fancied she heard his voice rising above the sound of revelry. She cried for much of the time – tears of grief. She could not imagine ever returning to that camp, to that man, and to Aaron's ridiculous golden calf. She felt that she should rescue her children, especially Enan and Sarai, but somehow she couldn't move.

On the second afternoon, with unaccountable intuition, Rachael turned round to see what Zipporah was doing. Zipporah, too, had spent the previous night huddled under a cloak. Now she and her children were on their feet, excitedly pointing to something up the mountain. Rachael strained her eyes in the same direction.

Her defeated emotions boiled into instant joy. Two figures were walking with swift purpose down the mountain – one grey-haired, the other young. The older man was carrying something which occasionally reflected the fading sunlight. From time to time, they would stop and peer beyond Rachael and Zipporah towards the centre of the Israelite camp, where the party was still throbbing. Moses and Joshua strode on again, paused again, walked again. They seemed in a hurry to make out what exactly was happening in the camp.

Rachael turned to look behind her. From her elevated position on the roots of the mountain, she easily made out the shifting shapes of people dancing around the shining form of Aaron's calf. Surely next time Moses stopped he would discover what was happening.

Rachael could now see clearly what Moses was carrying: two thin, oval slices of dark, polished rock, perfectly smooth and flat on their faces but around the edge as rough and irregular as any rock on that fearful mountain. These were what she had longed for; the only thing that could bring an end to the Israelites' madness and Boaz's stupidity. These were God's instructions.

She ran to meet Moses, disregarding the abandoned boundary he had set around the mountain so many weeks before. She ran upwards, forcing her body to carry her up the rocky track.

Moses stopped again.

Rachael slowed to a walk. She was close enough see the script carved across the slithers of rock…the most beautiful she had ever seen… far beyond the craftsmanship of any Egyptian stonemason. She stopped and stared open-mouthed at its beauty. Her heart swelled. This was not the work of any man or woman.

Moses' face suddenly changed, draining white with fury. Rachael knew why. She looked again at the engraved stones. The simple grace of the script, the delicate detail of each letter, the faultless balance of the design – left her numb with wonder.

Moses lifted one of the stones and studied it. Tears flooded from his eyes. His mouth twisted into a grimace of utter grief.

Then – it all happened in a moment – he lifted the stone slice higher, above the level of his gaze. His grip on the dark polished rock was firm, not reverential but determined.

Rachael understood instantly what he intended to do.

Moses raised the first five of God's commandments above his shoulder, now struggling to hold them steady in one hand.

Rachael broke into a run.

He raised the stone higher than his head, his face resolute.

Rachael screamed, 'NOOOOOOO!'

She was too late.

Moses lost control of the first stone, pushing it to the ground with all his strength.

Rachael tripped and tumbled to the ground. As God's own handiwork shattered into tiny fragments on the rough mountain path, so did her hopes. She raised her grazed, dust-smeared face from the ground in time to see Moses raise the second stone slice into the air, now using both hands, and smash it to pieces with all the force he could muster.

They were gone. God's ten, life-shaping words – smashed.

Israel did not deserve such a precious gift. The world would never see those beautiful words, inscribed by God. At that moment, Rachael, if she could, would have simply died, there on God's mountain.

But she didn't.

A SMALL, SMOOTH STONE

'WHAT DO YOU want?' the huge bulk of Philistia's most famous soldier grunted.

'It's time to get up, sir,' his shield bearer suggested cautiously.

The tone of the servant's voice betrayed controlled fear. Waking Goliath was like disturbing a sleeping bear. One swipe from his fist could kill a man, and had done more than once.

'I get up when the trumpet goes,' the celebrated fighter grumbled, pulling a blanket over his head.

The shield bearer instinctively reached forward to pull the blanket back, but stopped himself. Instead, he raised his voice very slightly. 'The trumpet has already gone, sir. You must have slept through it... ' Then, unseen by his master and illustrated by an upward roll of his eyes, he mouthed, '... again.'

Goliath's close-shaven head erupted from his bed. The shield bearer darted backwards. The champion bellowed, 'Well, I didn't hear it.'

For a moment the background murmur of the Philistine battle camp was hushed.

Everybody knew that voice.

Shebner the shield bearer returned carefully to within striking distance of his master's remarkably long arms and waited for a moment. He had served this vain brute for five years, far longer than any of his predecessors – most of whom had retired through serious injury. He knew how to handle him.

'I thought I heard it, sir, but I'll go and check.'

'I thought I heard it, sir,' Goliath mocked, imitating the tone of his servant's voice.

Shebner allowed himself a knowing smile at this mockery. He had survived his five years in Goliath's service because he was clever – clever enough to ensure that Goliath had no idea how clever he was. Masters, the world over, assume that they are smarter than those who serve them; good servants know better than to unsettle this assumption. Goliath did not know that every evening, after the few minutes he gave routinely to sharpening his sword and javelin, Shebner spent as many hours doing the same thing, because he knew that his own life relied on those razor edges. Goliath did not know that Shebner paid extra, from his own purse, to have Goliath's wine watered down before it was delivered, because Shebner knew the value of his master's good balance and swift reactions. And Shebner would never let Goliath know that a few moments earlier he had persuaded the duty trumpeter to blow the morning alarm-call right outside the great man's tent.

Goliath was a man who had to win, no matter what the contest. Shebner knew that even though he could win comfortably any battle of wits against his master, he would never survive the victory.

Shebner backed out of the tent and nodded to the waiting trumpeter. Bleary-eyed soldiers around the camp were mildly surprised to hear reveille sound for a second time, but continued their preparations for war. Shebner mouthed his thanks to the trumpeter and returned to his master's immaculate and expensive tent.

Goliath had the best of everything; it was his reward for being the single most important weapon in the King of Philistia's armoury. His houses were beautiful. His clothes were beautiful. His wives were beautiful – most of them, at least. He was in the habit of celebrating each successful battle with a new wife. Whenever possible he took the widow of the man – king, prince or general – he had just slaughtered.

However, despite his wealth and importance to Philistia's national security, Goliath was bored. And boredom was an experience he found hard to endure.

The Philistine army was carrying out a campaign against one of their traditional enemies, the Israelites. It was a campaign they usually won. But, even though the two armies had drawn up their battle lines every day for several weeks, not a single Israelite had been killed. That was frustrating. Killing people was the one thing Goliath was really good at. It was what kept him at the pinnacle of Philistine society.

He had already endured the forced inactivity of winter. Now it was spring – the time for war – and the great champion was desperate for his first kill of the season. But the Israelites did not want to fight. They did not want to fight because they knew they would lose. So, to replace the primeval thrill of watching Philistia's enemies die on the end of his spear, Goliath drank wine. Each evening, as the insecurity of idleness deepened, so did his need for unquestioning oblivion.

Shebner understood this. But each morning it was getting harder and harder to rouse his master from sleep. Perhaps today the real fighting would begin.

The Philistine army was camped above the Valley of Elah. Across the valley was the significantly smaller camp of the Israelites. Every day for almost six weeks Goliath had demanded that the Israelite king provide a champion to meet him in single combat. Today was the fortieth day of this stand-off, and not one Israelite soldier had accepted the invitation. The deal was simple: whoever won the single combat would win the war. It was a way of avoiding Philistine deaths and the political inconvenience they caused.

The Israelites knew they could not match the size and fighting efficiency of the Philistine army; they had no choice but to accept Goliath's terms. But they also knew Goliath's record. He had never been beaten in battle. Every one of his previous fighting partners was dead. He had won extensive territory and wealth for his king, his country and himself. He was the tallest man anyone had ever seen. His height and strength were legendary. The Israelites had no one to match him, and they knew it.

Goliath loved single combat. He liked to play with his victims. He kept them deliberately at bay until he had worked out which weapon they considered to be their best. Then he would employ the same weapon to destroy them. If they thought of themselves as swordsmen, he hacked them to pieces with his sword; if they preferred to keep their distance and throw a javelin – a sensible option against so tall an opponent – he was just as happy to skewer them his own custom-built, armour-piercing, solid bronze missile.

However, throughout this Israelite campaign, the only things Goliath had thrown were insults. He was tired of waiting.

Shebner looked into his master's bloodshot eyes. He spoke gently. 'Two kings and two armies are waiting for you, sir.'

'That feels better.' Goliath purred deeply as he stepped out in front of the Philistine battle line. He felt at home with his helmet fitted snugly over his head, his scale armour clinging to his chest, and two thick metal greaves strapped to his legs. Standing there, cocooned in bronze, with the strongest army in the region behind him, he was safe. It was an exhilarating safety, quite unlike the dull security of home. It was the safety of an eagle as it plummets towards its prey, confident that the flesh about to be breached is another's. Goliath was further reassured by the pale fear adorning every face in the Israelite battle line.

Maybe today one of those hairy immigrants would accept his challenge. Maybe tonight he would be toasting victory rather than drowning frustration.

'King Saul has upped the reward for any of his men who faces you,' Shebner said casually, carefully preparing his master for another long and fruitless wait.

'What's he offering?' Goliath's eyes sparkled at the thought of battle. 'A state funeral?'

He laughed. The Israelites amused him. They could talk a good battle with stories about their god, who had once single-handedly obliterated the Egyptian army. But standing there in the Valley of Elah, clutching their home-made weapons, they presented a negligible threat. How could such a weak people boast such a strong god?

Goliath's shoulders heaved as he laughed, causing the polished scales of his armour to shimmer in the sunlight. There was no inducement that King Saul could offer that would compensate for an Israelite champion's certain death.

Shebner, standing in his master's shadow, laughed politely.

'King Saul has thrown his own daughter into the reward pot.'

'Is she tasty?'

'I haven't a clue.'

'Make sure I get her when I win.'

Shebner nodded to note the instruction.

Goliath laughed again. 'Even if she looks like a hippopotamus' foot, I can find a use for her.'

He ran his eye along the Israelite battle line. It unnerved them to see him laughing. He liked that.

'Remind me what I'm worth now,' he demanded of his shield bearer.

'Total exemption from taxes for the victor and all his family, and now a royal wedding.'

Goliath smiled with childish satisfaction.

Shebner added, 'Saul's desperate.'

The gladiator flashed with anger. 'So am I. Standing here like a prize peacock every day.'

'Be patient, sir,' Shebner soothed. 'The Israelites know they can't beat us in open battle. They have to put someone up to face you.'

'I hate waiting!' Goliath was beginning to shout.

Across the valley, the Israelites went quiet. They knew what was coming next. They had endured it twice a day, every day, for more than a month.

'Why do you bother lining up for battle?' Goliath roared at them. 'You never fight!' He grabbed his heavy, iron-tipped spear from Shebner's hand and lifted it effortlessly into the air. 'Choose a man and send him down here. If he can kill me, all Philistia will be yours.' Goliath waited for the mocking cheer he knew would come from the Philistine troops behind him. As it began to fade, he continued, 'But when I kill your champion…' Shebner raised a hand to quiet the Philistine defiance – this was a practised piece of military theatre. In the sickly silence, Goliath concluded, '… you will become our slaves.'

Goliath watched as the poorly armed Israelite peasants did what they always did: looked nervously at one another, talking with lowered voices and darting eyes. It was a small victory to cause such dismay; he would rather spill some blood.

'I defy you,' he howled greedily. 'Give me a man, and let us FIGHT.'

Shebner flinched. He did not like the note of desperation in his master's voice. Desperation could lead to carelessness, and carelessness in a soldier could be fatal.

Goliath plunged the shaft of his spear into the ground, whereupon many of the Israelite soldiers raised their arms to heaven in prayer.

'Don't think your god will save you,' Goliath roared. If this was the only sport he was going to get today, he was determined to enjoy it. 'Your invisible god is useless here. You need a real god or – better still – someone who can actually fight.'

Goliath liked to mock the religions of his enemies. It always annoyed them. He had very little time for the fancy rituals of the Philistine priests; he had none at all for the daft practices of his enemies. And, when it came to religion, the Israelites were the daftest. They didn't even have a temple. They kept their shapeless, nameless god in a shabby old tent.

Suddenly he was bored again.

Shebner was quick to respond to his master's distinctive nasal sigh. 'You stirred them up well today, sir.' He needed to keep Goliath's mind positive. A moment later, he spotted an unusual flurry of activity in one section of the Israelite line.

'See that, sir?' he pointed. 'It might be your lucky day.'

At midday the two armies, as always, returned to their tents to escape the hottest hours of the afternoon. While the rest of the Philistine army were happily eating, gambling, arguing and bullying, the talisman of their confidence slipped morosely and alone into his silk-lined tent. Shebner knew that it would require extra tact and diplomacy to get his master out onto the battlefield for the evening face-off. He busied himself with routine tasks.

Goliath was onto his second skinful of wine when the news came. There was a barely perceptible change in the noise that filled the valley. But there was a rumour. Then messages arrived from Philistine spies in the Israelite camp. Someone had been tempted by King Saul's offer of a royal bride. The Israelites finally had a challenger to face Goliath. Confirmation of this news came to Shebner from his own king's shield bearer. Goliath's shield bearer could not help feeling excited. He was a soldier too. Defeating the Israelites was something to look forward to.

He arrived at Goliath's tent, short of breath from running, and began the delicate task of coaxing the half-empty skin of secretly diluted wine from his master's hand.

'You might have someone to fight this afternoon,' he informed Goliath. The 'might' was important. He knew what would happen if he built up the champion's hopes too far, and they crashed.

'You say that every day,' the big man mumbled through his neatly trimmed beard.

Goliath was feeling sorry for himself.

'There are reports—' Shebner began.

'Reports!' Goliath dismissed him. 'I can't fight a report.'

Shebner tried again. 'King Saul has nominated a challenger.'

'Has a formal challenge been made?'

'Not yet. But—'

'You can take this wine off me when there is a formal challenge.'

This was the kind of single combat that Shebner excelled at. Once in a while Shebner could get away with treating the famous warrior as his son. Their respective ages would have allowed such a relationship, though their relative sizes made it unlikely.

'Goliath, sir, if there is a genuine challenger, you will need a clear head.'

Goliath responded with a loud and deliberate belch.

Shebner continued, 'Hand me the wine, for now. I will give it back if no formal challenge is made within the hour.'

Goliath eyed his shield bearer cautiously. 'How do I know you will give it back?'

'If I don't, you can charge the whole skinful against my wages.'

'This is expensive wine.'

Shebner did not remove his gaze from his employer's eyes. He knew the price of the wine better than Goliath did. He replied, coolly, 'I can afford it.'

'I pay you too much.'

Shebner held out his hand.

A trumpet sounded, calling the Philistine soldiers back to their battle line.

Goliath passed the wineskin to his shield bearer.

As his nation's undisputed champion, Goliath was always the last to take up his position on the battlefield. He waited, motionless in this tent, soaking in the familiar sound of clanging weapons and scurrying feet. There was a hum of excitement. The rumour of a challenger had infused the Philistine army. Men who had strapped their helmets to their heads needlessly for the past five weeks were chattering eagerly about what they would do with their share of the victors' loot. Goliath relished the tingle of excitement in his chest. Shebner slowly moved the hard-won skin of wine out of his master's reach, listening for the swift patter of a messenger's feet weaving through the heavy plod of passing soldiers. At last it came.

'The king requests the presence of LORD Goliath,' the young messenger announced through the gold-braided tent entrance.

'Is there a challenge?' the huge man shouted impatiently from inside.

'I have not been told, sir,' the messenger replied uncertainly.

Goliath roared with irritation.

The youth took two involuntary steps backwards.

Shebner glared at the young man, demanding more information.

'The king has received ambassadors from King Saul of Israel.'

'Is there a formal challenge?' Goliath bellowed. He did not want hints and politics. He wanted to fight and to win, to sit back in his tent with aching limbs and blood – someone else's – on his hands.

Shebner waved the messenger aside.

'If you go to the king, sir, he will tell you about the challenge.' Again he employed his humble but uncompromising stare.

'Get my weapons,' Goliath conceded aggressively.

Shebner was ready for action.

Goliath strode proudly through the camp. Shebner, following two calculated paces behind, had to trot occasionally to keep up, so long were the big man's strides. Everyone they passed steered out of Goliath's way, bowing their heads respectfully towards the national icon. As they reached the centre of the camp, they passed the shrines of the Philistine gods. Shebner paused and bowed reverently. Goliath did not. He knew that he was the true object of Philistia's worship. He was the one on whom the people's lives and futures depended. They could offer as many sacrifices as they wished to their gods, but it was his spear, sword and javelin that really protected them, that brought them the unprecedented wealth and security they enjoyed.

He marched straight on.

When he came to his king's tent – a less affluent affair than his own – he hardly broke his step. He marched straight in, giving no signal of respect to his monarch. The only thing that caused Goliath to bow was the low roof; it was a long time since he had bowed to his king.

The king was a worshipper too; no less dependent on the size, strength and skill of Goliath of Gath than anyone else.

The champion stood uncomfortably, his head pushing up into the tent's roof. There were two Israelite ambassadors awaiting his arrival.

'Well?' he demanded, addressing the king as he might speak to any soldier in the Philistine ranks.

'You have a challenger,' the king informed him, tolerating his rudeness.

'Who?'

An Israelite ambassador stepped forward stiffly. 'David of Bethlehem, the son of Jesse.'

'Never heard of him!'

There was silence.

The ambassador turned to the king. 'I will inform King Saul of your terms.' The two ambassadors bowed and left.

'So?' Goliath demanded as soon as the sound of Israelite armour had faded into the clatter of the camp. 'Who is this David of Bethlehem?'

'Apparently an honoured champion of King Saul.' The king's voice was thick with irony as he quoted the official line from the Israelite ambassadors. 'He is a fresh branch of the house of Israel, a slayer of lions and bears.'

'What does that mean?'

Shebner read between the diplomatic lines. 'It means that he is a young man who has never taken part in a battle in his life.'

The king stared at Shebner, a little surprised by the accuracy of the servant's insight.

'And the lions and bears?' Goliath demanded.

'My sources tell me,' the king volunteered, 'that David of Bethlehem is a thirteen-year-old shepherd who arrived in the Israelite camp this morning to deliver ten cheeses to his older brothers.'

Goliath began to giggle which, his head pushing into the roof, shook the entire structure of the tent. After all the weeks of waiting, this eventual absurdity slipped beneath his guard. 'When I have flattened the boy,' he chortled, 'I want every one of those ten cheeses for myself.'

Sagely, the king nodded his agreement. He was about to take possession of the entire wealth of Israel; he could afford a little cheese. He humoured his champion with a patient smile.

Goliath looked down on Shebner and chortled, 'Cheeses at twenty paces. Is it possible to kill a man with a— '

There was a sharp pain in his foot. Shebner was treading, quite deliberately, on his toes. Goliath looked into the stern eyes of his shield bearer. There was no fuel for laughter in that weathered face.

When Goliath's breathing had finally returned to normal, Shebner stepped off his master's foot and out into the sunlight. The tall champion stooped through the doorway after him.

Outside, in the dusty heat of the Philistine camp, the shield bearer stood, a polished shield in one hand, an iron-tipped spear in the other.

'An unknown opponent,' he stated icily, 'is an unknown danger.'

'He's thirteen years old!' Goliath declared, as if that settled the matter.

'When did you last fight a thirteen-year-old shepherd?'

Goliath stared at his servant, unable to believe that there was anything in this situation worth taking seriously.

'You have never fought a thirteen-year-old shepherd,' Shebner informed him, his voice laced with anger. 'And so you do not know how a thirteen-year-old shepherd fights.' Then he repeated his homespun proverb: 'An unknown opponent is an unknown danger.'

Shebner fought his emotions. If – just if – the champion of the Philistines were to meet his match that day, he – Shebner – would be the very next person cut down by the victorious Israelites. He never took such prospects lightly.

'We need to get out in front of the battle line as soon as we reasonably can,' he advised sternly. 'Then we can get a good look at David of Bethlehem and assess the danger he presents.'

The soldiers in the Israelite line looked no less pale and nervous than they had under Goliath's verbal bombardment earlier that day.

'You see,' Goliath probed his shield bearer, brimful with confidence, 'they don't believe in David of Bethlehem any more than I do.'

Shebner said nothing. He could see the fear on the Israelites' faces. What frightened him was his master's complacency.

There was a ripple of activity further up the stream which ran between the two lines of opposing soldiers. A small group of senior Israelite officers had left their camp and were gathered beside the water.

'Is he with that lot?' Goliath asked.

'I don't know,' Shebner replied, 'but I think he might be.'

'Let's take a closer look.'

'Not yet, sir.'

The Israelite officers were standing in a loose circle looking down into the stream. It was not possible to see what they were looking at.

'They're probably making an offering to the god of the stream,' Goliath suggested dismissively.

'Israelites don't do things like that.' Shebner was alert to all possible dangers, and anything unusual was a potential danger. He was desperate to know what the Israelite leaders were doing there.

The group broke up and began to walk downstream towards Goliath. Through the line of experienced soldiers and into view stepped a red-haired youth dressed in a woollen tunic with a small leather pouch slung over his shoulder.

'Is that him?' Goliath began to giggle again.

'You can laugh as much as you like…' Shebner responded sharply, 'when you have killed him. Until then, an unknown— '

'I know, I know,' the champion silenced his shield bearer. 'I want a closer look at him.'

Both lines of soldiers went silent the moment Goliath moved. The Philistine troops began to drum their spear shafts against the dry earth, making the ground tremble beneath the feet of their opponents.

The combat had begun. Shebner was fully alert. Goliath, now sober and serious, slipped quickly into the familiar routine of battle: studying his enemy, searching for obvious strengths and evident weaknesses, awake to the slightest clue. In this forum Goliath of Gath was an unrivalled genius.

The young shepherd's favoured weapon – in fact, his only weapon – was some kind of slingshot made from a curved stick and a leather strap. Goliath noted how steadily he gripped the stick. Usually, out of anxiety, a combatant would unconsciously and repeatedly refine their hold on their favoured weapon.

This boy was not nervous.

How dare he not be nervous! Anger flared through the Philistine.

'Am I a dog,' Goliath's deep voice echoed up the valley, 'that you come against me with a stick?'

His pride was wounded. King Saul was mocking him, sending a mere child to the fight. Before setting eyes on the youth, Goliath had intended to dispatch the Israelite challenger cleanly. But now he wanted to mash the boy, to rip him to pieces in front of the cowardly Israelites and their king.

'Come here,' Goliath roared. 'I will make you into dog food.'

'Sir!' Shebner barked sharply under his breath, without moving his lips. He needed to rein in Goliath's temper.

Goliath replied with an irritated snort.

Meanwhile, the bare-armed, barely armed shepherd stopped. He stood motionless, coolly surveying his towering opponent.

'You are coming against me with a sword and a spear,' David declared confidently. 'But I come against you in the name of the living God.'

'What god?' Goliath snapped back. 'There is no god.'

'The God of Israel will deliver you into my hands.' David's voice modulated in pitch as he shouted; it had not yet fully broken. 'I will strike you down today,' he informed the champion of Philistia. 'I will cut off your cursing head.'

'With a stick?' Goliath laughed as he said it.

Shebner shot out a warning cough from deep in his throat.

David stepped forwards, within striking distance of the giant. Was it just the brazen confidence of youth? Shebner could not remember a combat in which Goliath had faced an opponent who was not thoroughly terrified. David showed no hint of fear. His voice was rich with assurance as he replied quietly, 'No. I will cut off your head with your own sword.'

Goliath raised his famously heavy sword, snorted with derision, and returned it to its sheath. He turned to Shebner with a foolish grin. He did not understand this strange boy, but he knew he would be easy enough to kill.

Shebner gave his master a warning stare.

Suddenly Goliath's fragile self-restraint snapped. He gave in to an unruly cocktail of anger, amusement and uncertainty: anger at King Saul, amusement at the spotty youth and uncertainty because David showed no fear.

He snarled at the boy.

David looked steadily up into the warrior's eyes. 'When I am minding my father's sheep, and a lion or bear comes and carries off a sheep from the flock, I go after it and rescue the sheep from its mouth. If it turns on me, I kill it.'

This was unexpected. Goliath stared down at the lad, confused. He had to reply, and do so quickly. This war of words was part of the battle – part of the essential process of assessing the enemy.

'I am not a lion or a bear.'

'No.' David's reply was immediate. 'You are a godless Philistine.'

Goliath opened his mouth to reply to the taunt, but David did not give him the opportunity.

He went on, 'And the God who has protected me from the jaws of lions and bears will protect me from you.'

Goliath had heard enough. He chose his weapon. He had no sling to match the boy's favoured tool of war, but he would use his own stick – the thick wooden spear with its seven kilogram warhead. He snatched it from Shebner.

The two fighters backed away from one another to prepare themselves. Meanwhile, the valley was increasingly filled with hubbub – the violent chants of the Philistines and the fervent prayers of the Israelites.

Shebner matched his master's steps, holding out Goliath's thick shield.

Goliath glanced uncertainly at the brightly painted defence. He could not imagine needing it.

Shebner shoved it towards him insistently.

Goliath reluctantly reached out his left arm to take it. While this was happening, David did not move his gaze from Goliath's face, but steadily lowered his left hand into the leather pouch slung over his shoulder.

Shebner was about to bombard Goliath, one more time, with his proverb about unknown enemies. But it was too late.

Goliath let out a deep roar and charged at his prey.

The Philistine army cheered in anticipation.

David pulled a wet stone from the bag and slipped it into his sling.

The continued pounding of Philistine spear shafts shook the ground.

David held his ground; he did not move his gaze from Goliath's eyes.

Goliath closed in.

Shebner held his breath.

Goliath shifted his grip on his spear.

David spun the sling above his head.

Goliath lowered the spear, directing its gleaming tip at the youth's unprotected heart.

David released his stone.

Goliath charged onwards, wondering how many stones David had in that bag.

David lowered his arm.

Goliath pounded on.

David smiled.

Goliath told himself, 'My spear will skewer this child like a— '

Thud.

A MAN YOU CAN TRUST

'YOU HAVE TO trust somebody,' Artaxia told her husband, her tone reprimanding.

King Darius was not so sure.

Darius had been involved in the business of war and politics for many years. He had seen too many people toppled from power by those they had trusted. The secret of kingship, it seemed to him, was to trust no one. But it was stiflingly lonely at the very top of the political tree.

He looked across the decadent glamour of the royal bedroom to his beautiful young wife. Silent attendants were preparing her for her husband's bed.

Of course she wanted to be trusted. She was full of idealistic zeal for her role in uniting the Babylonians and the Medes; she believed that her marriage to the silver-haired king could bring an end to generations of tribal tension.

But Darius was too old to see life so simply. He had come to supreme power late in life. He was sixty-two. His predecessor had fallen victim of an unremarkable coup in which several generals united to murder their monarch and share the blame. But that is where their unity had ended. In the vacuum that followed they discovered that no one of them was satisfactorily trusted by the others to take the vacant throne. And so Darius was called on: a retired general, a seasoned politician, a 'safe pair of hands', and – given his age – not likely to occupy the seat of power for too long.

'You trust me, darling, don't you?' Artaxia asked innocently, turning wide, dark eyes towards the man who was waiting in the bed.

Darius prided himself on his honesty, so he did not answer the question. Their marriage was a political necessity, not an act of love. Darius had had many lovers and it was a joy, at his age, to share his bed with such a beautiful young woman. But he had married her only because her father was the man he trusted least of all the regional rulers.

'You look so beautiful, my love,' he replied, switching to a more comfortable truth. 'Come to bed now.'

An hour later, Darius lay awake. Artaxia was right. He had to trust someone. He could not keep watch over a hundred and twenty regional rulers on his own. He had to form an inner circle of power. Artaxia's father had to be part of it; he was far too dangerous to remain just one of the hundred and twenty. The other inevitable candidate was Darius' former deputy, Cyrazzar, who had sponsored him for the kingship. Cyrazzar and Artaxia's father Buchnachaz were political opposites and highly unlikely to unite against him. Darius needed someone else – a diverting dynamic – someone independent, who would distract the two generals from their differences; someone wise; someone who, like him, understood the complexities of politics and looked down on them; someone he could truly trust.

He lay awake half the night, occasionally breaking off from affairs of state to marvel at the vision of natural beauty sleeping beside him.

Was there anyone in his kingdom who did not lust for power?

Over and over again, Darius ran through his memories of King Belshazzar's downfall. The man had become complacent. He had fallen into the trap of believing in his own wealth. But the influential and industrious merchants who generated Babylon's wealth did not want an idle king. Belshazzar's idleness did nothing to protect their edge in the world's markets. They bought the allegiance of the generals and had the complacent king removed. Darius, in his turn, had bought the allegiance of the merchants by offering them limited amounts of lucrative power.

He muttered into the warm night, 'There has to be someone who is honest.'

The king climbed out of bed and walked silently to the great hall where Belshazzar had held his fateful, final feast a few months earlier. He stood there remembering his predecessor's last night alive. Darius had been there: a silent observer… an interested silent observer. The net was already closing around the royal fool, but then a mysterious, disembodied hand had appeared, high up on the palace wall. Women had screamed, war-hardened generals had vomited into their suppers, while the hand silently scribed strange icons across the painted plaster. The script was still there, just visible in the glow of the orange torch flames. The lines and curves of the foreign text meant nothing to Darius, even now. But he remembered the interpretation given by the one man in all Babylon able to read the inscription.

'Mene' – your number is up.

'Tekel' – you are a lightweight.

'Peres' – you are sliced in two.

King Belshazzar was not actually sliced in two – a dagger in the heart had dealt with him – but his kingdom was. Darius had only been entrusted with half an empire.

Darius stood in the torchlight, remembering the white-haired immigrant who had interpreted this doom-laden prophecy. The man had been offered both wealth and power in return for solving the embarrassing mystery. But he had turned it down. He had stood there, his faded robes suggesting someone who had once been significant, and plainly rejected the king's gifts. It was enough for him – so he said – to speak the truth.

Darius returned to his bed. He would enquire further about the old man in the morning. For now, he pressed himself close up to his smooth-skinned queen and slept.

It was not a simple thing for a king to visit the home of an ordinary citizen in his capital city. Such an outing required bodyguards and royal secretaries – people who fussed and worried. Darius resented it. A few weeks ago he could have walked alone through the crowded streets and knocked on Daniel's door with his own fist. But not any longer.

A young servant girl opened the door. She was a foreigner.

A senior secretary announced the king's arrival.

The girl explained, politely and charmingly, 'You will have to wait, sir. My master is praying.'

'The king is here,' the secretary laboured, raising his voice over any language barrier that might have stood between them. He stepped aside and pointed to Darius. 'The king is here to see Daniel, now.'

'I understand that, sir,' she said calmly. 'But my master is praying.' She looked apologetically towards Darius, seeking some understanding.

Darius was impressed. One could learn a great deal about a man from the manner of his servants. He liked the girl's confidence. He was all the more interested in meeting Daniel.

'May we wait inside?' he asked casually.

She flushed a little. 'Certainly, your majesty. I regret that we are not prepared for your comfort.'

Darius could not resist a slight smile, though it was against his principles to smile at servants without very good reason. 'Just a little shade in a place where I am less likely to be run down by horses will suffice,' he replied.

They were ushered into a modest, sparsely decorated room. There was only one chair, on which lay a clutch of parchment scrolls. The girl looked at them but did nothing. She did not have the authority to move them, even for the King of Babylon.

There was an uneasy silence.

'At which temple does your master pray?' Darius asked.

'He doesn't, sir,' she said, her eyes darting involuntarily to the scrolls on the chair.

'Where does a man pray if he does not go to a temple?'

'Master Daniel prays upstairs, your majesty.' Her voice was unsteady; she was not sure whether it was her place to say such things, but neither could she refuse to answer the king. 'He is a Jew, sir, from the holy city of Jerusalem.'

'I have heard of the Jews,' Darius continued. 'They used to worship an invisible god in a temple with no image.' He paused thoughtfully, then added, 'King Nebuchadnezzar destroyed it.'

Darius had only recently been reminded of this story. On the evening of Belshazzar's death, the vain king had shown off the articles of gold and silver which Nebuchadnezzar had captured from the Jewish god's temple.

The servant girl said nothing.

'Are you a Hebrew too?' the king asked her.

She nodded solemnly.

The silence was awkward. The secretaries huffed and sighed at being made to wait by a man who was upstairs and who must surely know by now that the king was present. Darius reflected on the girl's sadness, and on the personal tragedy that was the inevitable companion to any empire's growth.

Eventually they heard sounds of movement from the room above them: a window being closed… soft footsteps… a door opening and closing. Daniel appeared.

Darius dismissed his entourage to the outer courtyard. He did not trust them. In his own palace he would have supplied music to entertain them, to ensure that they could not overhear any private conversations. Here, in Daniel's home, he had to trust to the privacy afforded by two cedarwood doors and the noise from the nearby marketplace.

'Allow me to provide you with food and drink, your majesty.' Daniel offered the traditional courtesies of host to guest.

Darius nodded graciously.

'I am afraid that in this household we drink only water and eat only vegetables and fruit.'

An anxious look flickered across the king's face. Even in the countryside, drinking water was a health lottery played by peasants. In the city, it was an open invitation to disease.

Daniel was familiar with the Babylonians' sensitivities concerning his frugal diet. He bowed slightly towards the king, explaining, 'I collect my own water in my own cistern during the winter rains. I can vouch for its purity.'

Darius nodded his acceptance of this warranty.

Daniel left the king alone; alone and thoughtful.

The white-haired Jew returned, carrying a tray on which were simple goblets carved from soft stone, a stone pitcher and a basket of fruit.

Darius noted that this man, who had at least one servant in his household, still fetched and carried these things. But neither man commented on the uncommonness of Daniel's behaviour.

⌒

That night, while Artaxia slept, Darius sat at his writing table, planning the administration of his kingdom. He was a man inspired. He had found what he was looking for – and more. In Daniel he had found a politician with decades of experience; he had found a man who had no time for the chaos and kerfuffle that the priests of Babylon called 'religion'; he had found someone who appeared unstained by the insatiable greed which drove Babylonian society to ever more excess.

But for one significant factor, Darius would have happily concluded that Daniel was a gift from the gods. That restraining factor was that Darius, King of Babylon, did not believe there were any gods. He had studied the machinations of human society for many years and knew that the driving force behind everything was not faith or fate, but old-fashioned selfishness. The two old men had discussed these matters for hours that day in the simple tranquility of Daniel's home, while the secretaries sweated obediently in the sun-flooded courtyard.

Darius would have stayed even longer but when Daniel noticed the first hint of afternoon shadow on his window ledge, he had made polite farewells to his king, picked up one of his precious scrolls and climbed the stairs to his upper room, to pray to the invisible god of the destroyed temple and of the defeated Jews.

'If that is what makes the man so honest,' Darius murmured in the flickering torchlight of his private chamber, 'I will happily put up with it.'

By the time Darius heard the muted shuffle of the palace guard changing in the middle of the night, his plan was complete and he was enjoying the warmth of his queen's body. He would maintain the one hundred and twenty regional rulers, though he would do his best to keep them independent of one another. Instead of gathering the regions into united provinces – which could become independently powerful – he would have the regional rulers directly overseen by three imperial administrators: Buchnachaz (his father-in-law), Cyrazzar (his patron) and Daniel.

⌒

The new system worked wonderfully. Darius was able to trust Artaxia enough for her to be happy, and that kept her father at heel. Buchnachaz was further distracted by the arrival of his royal grandchildren. Cyrazzar was easily tamed with occasional favourable references placed in the royal records.

Meanwhile, Daniel's experienced grasp of palace affairs made him an ever-reliable forecaster of real trouble. If Daniel informed the king that one particular regional ruler appeared to be gaining wealth rather more swiftly than anyone else in that region, further enquiry was always fruitful. Punishment was uncompromising. Such betrayals were handled using traditional Babylonian justice. The centrepiece symbol of royal supremacy over Babylonia was the palace's collection of wild lions. Enemies of the state from beyond the state – rival kings, for example – had their children slaughtered before their eyes, then immediately had their own eyes gouged out. Enemies of the state from within the state, however, were fed to the king's lions, along with their wives and children.

Darius was content to maintain this tradition. Brutal justice, he observed, was called upon less frequently than lenient justice. He had built up a reputation throughout his military career for being a man who did what he said he would do… though it never entered his mind, even in his darkest nightmares, that he might end up applying such savage justice to his new friend Daniel.

It is a common fault to assume that something which has been working well will continue to work well if it is maintained as it is. King Darius did not notice how Buchnachaz gradually became accustomed to his status as royal grandfather. Neither did he observe the subtle cooling of Cyrazzar's passion for reading his own name in official records. And so the king was not alert to the danger of promoting Daniel as singular ruler over his other two administrators, answerable only to himself.

Artaxia supported the move. It was a partial retirement plan which would allow Darius more leisure time to spend with his children, to prepare their young sons for kingship. Cyrazzar and Buchnachaz both formally approved this investment in the future of the dynasty. But before the formalities of this transfer of power were drawn up and approved, the two men had a change of heart.

The fear of those of other races is mostly a subtle prejudice, like a weed spreading below the surface of the soil. Dislike for those who are unarguably better people than we are is more obvious; and we are quick to extinguish the light that shows up the secrets of our dark lives.

It was in these things that Buchnachaz and Cyrazzar found a common bond. While their daily outward disagreements reassured Darius that all was well in his kingdom, they quietly united in their dislike for Daniel.

This new unity first became obvious when a regional ruler was caught by Daniel's watchful scrutiny. The distraught man appealed to the two administrators to divert their colleague's attention, while also making broad promises and whispering vague threats. It was enough.

Their plan had a veneer of honesty. They set themselves the task of applying the same scrutiny to Daniel as he applied to all one hundred and twenty of the regional rulers. They embarked on a detailed audit of his affairs: what he did with his money, how he followed up any promises he made; how he conducted his relationships with the regions under his oversight – particularly those with significant Jewish communities.

As it was obvious that Daniel only spent a tiny fraction of his income on himself, the plotters quickly assumed that he was quietly underwriting the resurgence of the Jewish race. They watched carefully when he passed small bundles of silver coins to the widows and orphans of the cities he visited. To pass illicit funds though such a diverse network of nobodies was an ingenious strategy. It created a trail that was immensely hard to follow. But Buchnachaz and Cyrazzar followed it. They employed a legion of spies to follow Daniel's army of couriers.

The spies watched for the moment when Daniel closed the upstairs window at which he prayed, morning, noon and sunset. They followed him as he went out into the narrow city streets to distribute his monthly salary. The spies split up and tailed the apparently random selection of the city's poor. The trail led them directly to the nearest market square where the precious silver was exchanged for bread and bargain portions of damaged fruit. Here the spies met their greatest challenge, to follow the assorted bakers and grocers, to see where the trail of Daniel's wealth led next. It led everywhere: to farms, to other markets, to private homes, to moneylenders and respected merchants.

Month after month the administrators' spies carried out this work, eventually compiling an expensive report. 'Daniel,' they declared without doubt, 'is an honest man.'

It was bad news.

'We'll never find any basis for charges against him,' Cyrazzar complained to Buchnachaz that evening over a goblet of the king's best wine, 'unless it has something to do with his religion.'

Darius was demonstrating the basics of archery to the tiny princes when it was announced that his two administrators had arrived to see him.

'Tell them to take their business to Daniel,' he instructed.

'It is, they say, a matter that applies directly to your majesty,' the messenger reported.

Darius was irritated.

'What is it?' he demanded as he marched into his audience chamber, still straightening the robes of state around his shoulders. He was surprised to discover that the room was quite full. The regional rulers had been assembled.

Cyrazzar and Buchnachaz were swift to avoid any embarrassment. They had practised this meeting many times in the privacy of their own homes. They needed a king who was ready to be flattered, not one who was flustered.

When the leader of the Babylonian Empire was settled in his seat, Buchnachaz raised the matter of the forthcoming anniversary of Darius' accession to the throne. He then proceeded to list the significant achievements of Darius' reign so far. This was accompanied at all points by encouraging nods and cheers from the regional rulers. Buchnachaz was careful to include in his list the brilliance of Darius' reorganisation of the kingdom. The regional rulers were quick to praise this policy, for it was the foundation of their power.

And in all this, Buchnachaz's praise of Daniel was meticulously measured.

'This is a record to be celebrated,' Cyrazzar declared as the murmur of loyal affirmation died down.

King Darius took the bait. He sat upright on his throne and nodded thoughtfully.

'In my studies of the royal annals,' Cyrazzar continued, 'I have found record of an ancient custom which we consider opportune for this occasion.'

Darius, who found the royal annals tedious, listened attentively.

'It was once customary,' Cyrazzar explained, 'for the kings of Babylon to declare a month during which all worship in the empire was addressed exclusively to themselves as a mark of the monarch's divine ancestry.'

Cyrazzar knew that this sentiment would raise little interest in the king, so he moved swiftly to his next point. 'While we understand that many of our traditions fit uncomfortably with the realities of today's empire, your majesty will be as aware as we are of the need for a Medan king to affirm the ancient customs of Babylon.'

Darius' eyes darted along the lines of regional rulers. He was well aware that his Medan blood was a loophole that could easily be exploited. He noted the confirmatory nods of the leaders from the outlying provinces and understood the importance of showing himself as a truly Babylonian monarch.

Buchnachaz seized the moment. He leaned close to his royal master and said quietly, 'Your majesty will appreciate that it would not have been possible to get the agreement of the Lord Daniel to such a proposal.'

Darius nodded.

Cyrazzar stepped forward with a pile of parchment sheets. 'Your majesty, we have all agreed that you should issue an edict that anyone who prays to any god or man during the next thirty days, except to you, shall be thrown into your lions' den.'

It was a wise plan. It would reinforce national unity and consolidate royal power; it would also silence certain regional mutterings. Lastly, it would keep Cyrazzar and Buchnachaz happy.

Darius approved it.

It was a busy day. There were a hundred and twenty edicts to sign and seal, one for each of the regions. These were countersigned by the regional rulers, many of whom took the opportunity of fitting a quick item of important business into the rare event of being at the same table as the king. As soon as the edicts were signed, Darius was taken to a banquet to mark the start of thirty days of imperial worship. Along with the sumptuous menu there was a programme of sacred dance in honour of the Divine Emperor. Though Darius had little interest in Babylonian sacred ritual, there was nonetheless plenty about the sacred dancing to capture his attention.

He slept well.

The next day as orange sunlight poured into his bedroom, Darius pondered the absurdity of the people of Babylon addressing their prayers to him. He couldn't hear them. He couldn't answer them. He walked to his window and surveyed his capital city, wondering if anyone was actually praying to him at that very moment. He pondered the futility of religion. Somewhere, he remembered, in all that jumble of housing, the old Jew Daniel would be at his window praying away to his invisible god who had been unable to prevent King Nebuchadnezzar from demolishing the temple in Jerusalem. What a shame, Darius reflected, that Daniel's religious foibles had kept him from enjoying the food, wine and dancing that everyone else had shared the previous night.

'You're deep in thought, my dear.' Queen Artaxia joined him at the window. 'Anyone who didn't know you might have thought you were praying.'

'If I were,' Darius replied with amusement, 'I would have been praying to myself.'

Artaxia laced a delicate arm around him. 'I worship you, my love.'

Darius was not in the mood for her worship. 'There's many a man out there,' he said, sweeping his arm across the skyline of the city, 'who would happily push a dagger into my back in order to win your worship for himself.'

He turned, alert to a sudden commotion in the palace. From what he could hear, Darius understood that someone was trying urgently to speak to him, and the royal secretaries were struggling to hold them back. He and Artaxia watched the door, waiting for the inevitable moment when their bedchamber would be breached.

Cyrazzar was the first through the door, closely followed by Buchnachaz.

'Your majesty,' Cyrazzar blurted breathlessly. Then, with Buchnachaz's hand tightly gripping his arm, he blushed brightly and said nothing more.

There were embarrassed splutterings from the pack of secretaries following them as the chaotic mob attempted to reverse out of the room.

Darius, aware that the focus of everyone's attention was a short distance behind him, turned and was amused to discover that, as the bedchamber door had swung open, Artaxia had shrugged off her night robe. Hence Cyrazzar's embarrassment and her father's hasty retreat.

'Very clever,' Darius muttered as he restored his queen's modesty after the bedroom door had been closed.

Darius made his way to the audience chamber, where the two administrators were waiting for him. They had recovered their composure and met the king's arrival with grave faces.

'Your majesty,' Buchnachaz began. Darius noted an unusual forcefulness in the tone of his voice. 'Did you or did you not publish a decree that during the next thirty days anyone who prays to any god or man except to you would be thrown into the lions' den?'

Darius' mental defences were instantly activated. This was a leading question. So… there had been an ulterior motive to yesterday's acclamations. He would have to be very careful in everything he said. He now knew that these two men, despite his best efforts, had joined forces against him.

Darius only had two, maybe three seconds to consider. In that fraction of time he could not understand what kind of trap he had been lured into. He had to talk. He gave a stock answer using a traditional saying: 'The decree stands in accordance with the laws of the Medes and Persians, which cannot be repealed.'

Neither of the administrators spoke.

Darius replayed his words in his mind. Had he said the right thing? It was important to be seen to be strong and consistent.

He looked defiantly into his father-in-law's eyes – a man younger than himself. Darius did not feel defiant, however. He was experiencing the fear that every soldier feels in the face of a battle.

Cyrazzar spoke. 'We have learned, your majesty, that a Jew who lives in the city is wilfully disregarding your decree.'

At the word 'Jew', Darius was immediately transported to Daniel's simple home, with its vegetable garden and its precious scrolls. The king's stomach churned. Let it not be Daniel! Before he could stop himself, he was silently praying: 'O righteous gods, let it not be Daniel.'

Darius held Cyrazzar's gaze. Whatever panic might be raging in his mind, he would not give these odious men the pleasure of even a flicker of a royal eyelid.

Cyrazzar was obliged to continue. 'This man was observed last evening, praying to his defeated deity within an hour of reading your decree.'

Darius now knew where this was leading. There was only one Jew who would have had access to the decree so soon after its publication.

Buchnachaz joined the prosecution. 'And this morning, your majesty, the same Jew was at his window again, praying towards the ruined temple of Jerusalem.'

Darius battled to maintain his dignity, yet he felt faint. He walked slowly and purposefully towards the wooden throne and sat. Struggling to regain control of his body, he looked to his two administrators, waiting for them to deliver their final blow.

The administrators looked at each other. Neither of them wanted to speak first, neither wanted to be the one to complete this long-planned assault on their injured king. Their reluctance gave Darius an opportunity to reconsider his initial response. The words 'which cannot be repealed' pierced his soul like a fishbone stuck in the throat.

Cyrazzar administered the inevitable punch line: 'It was the LORD Daniel, your majesty.'

Darius was a shrewd veteran of numerous inquests and interrogations. He had only survived to see that day because he was always ready to defend himself. But now he was trapped; he was well trapped. He studied the frightened faces of the two men and recalled the events of the past day. He could not help admiring the symmetry of their plot. Yet he was utterly determined to confound it.

Darius' queasiness was over. He had assessed his enemy and was ready to fight. He would save Daniel. He would not allow malicious politics to overcome plain honesty, not in his kingdom. He dismissed the two plotters, telling them he would meet with them again at sunset. They would have to wait and worry; they deserved that. Then he made his way directly to the royal archive. Despite the saying, there had to be some precedent in the history of the Medes and the Persians for a law – an unjust law, a malicious law – to be repealed. Darius resolved to find it.

The king worked alone throughout the whole day. He dispatched his secretaries on mundane tasks and had his imperial guards prevent anyone from entering the palace library. He could not afford to share his quest.

It was depressing work. He found plenty of ludicrous laws – including one detailing the required course of action should a man give birth to a child – but none of them had been repealed, only allowed to lapse. Were it not for the desperate circumstances, it would have made entertaining reading. But the life of the only man he truly trusted was at stake, and he could not allow the laws of his own kingdom to carry out such a blatant injustice.

The library door never opened. Darius neither ate nor drank. At times he shouted at the unhearing scrolls. More than once he crashed his grey head onto the desk in despair. What he had said so carelessly appeared to be unerringly true: the laws of the Medes and Persians had never been repealed.

As the sun sank inconsiderately towards the Babylonian skyline, meticulous care gave way to panic. Showing no respect for the royal records, Darius grabbed at scrolls, scanned them for just the one word, 'repealed', and then threw them to the floor.

More and more frequently, he glanced out of the window. He cursed the sun. His despair blinded him. At the last, Darius did not even pause to read the scrolls but hurled them furiously across the room. Then, as the burning orb made contact with the city's blameless roofs, Darius straightened, pulled his robes into position and marched icily out of his library.

Buchnachaz and Cyrazzar were waiting for him. They were nervous – and they had good cause to be. They knew where their king had spent his day. They knew how he felt about Daniel. They knew that if it was not going to be Daniel's flesh filling the bellies of the royal lions that evening, it would be their own.

Darius was inscrutable. He stood at the window of his audience chamber and looked across the glowing city.

'It is sunset,' he declared. 'At sunset, Daniel prays to his god. Go directly to his house, taking a detachment of the Imperial Guard. If Daniel is no longer contravening my decree, I will have mercy on him.'

Darius stared in the direction of Daniel's home with no hope that such mercy would be required.

'But if you find him praying to his foreign god, bring him here. He will be fed to the lions.'

They went.

Darius waited.

Never before had he hated religion so desperately.

Cyrazzar and Buchnachaz were prepared for victory. They had arranged for a stone to be cut to cover the mouth of the lions' cave. They had also brought sealing wax so that the stone could be sealed in place and marked with both the king's and their own insignia. They were taking no risks.

Daniel was manacled and gagged like a dangerous criminal.

The king insisted that these indignities be removed. He also insisted that his prime minster be lowered to the floor of the cave carefully, not thrown in.

'The sentence,' he declared impassively, 'is that he be fed to the lions, not that his body be smashed on the rocks of their den.'

As Daniel stood there – silent, dignified, accepting of his punishment – Darius contemplated how rightly he had assessed the quality of this man. He could not comprehend Daniel's devotion to his god, but he knew courage when he saw it. He glanced at the two conspirators. They showed nothing of Daniel's dignity, though they were undoubtedly clever – cleverer than Darius had anticipated. He felt crushed. He had always believed that honesty would ultimately prevail over guile. But, at that moment, his faith was shattered. What else was there to believe in?

A rope was tied around Daniel's chest and he was lifted through the narrow opening above the lions' cave. As the old Jew's head disappeared from sight, Darius called out impulsively, 'Daniel, may your god rescue you.'

With every metre the rope was lowered, Cyrazzar and Buchnachaz stood taller. Then the rope went slack and the loose end was tossed down into the darkness.

The royal lions grunted and barked at the intrusion.

Cyrazzar and Buchnachaz gave instructions for the newly cut stone to be placed over the hole and hot wax was poured around its edges. Struggling to contain their pleasure, they produced their brass seals and pushed them into the setting wax.

Darius, soberly, did the same. The two administrators had won this battle, but he was determined not to let them win another. He thanked them curtly for their thoroughness and withdrew to his private rooms.

That night there was a second banquet to mark the celebrations of Darius' deity. He did not attend. He did not eat. He did not drink. He did not visit his wife.

He cursed the gods he did not believe in. He paced angrily round his room. And he tried very hard not to imagine the scene of the lions picking over the bones of his friend.

His friend!

Darius had long ago sacrificed the possibility of real friendship in pursuit of his career. Yet now – too late – he realised that true friendship had visited him. He remembered the first delightful conversation the two men had enjoyed together and the many that followed it. He interrogated his own mind, asking if he regretted the friendship that had grown between them. He could not persuade himself that he did. Daniel was a truly honest man, just as Buchnachaz and Cyrazzar were truly dishonest. He could not criticise himself for favouring truth over blatant self-interest.

He could not sleep.

In the dull, colourless first light of day, King Darius returned to the library. In his frenzy the previous evening he had spotted Daniel's name in the annals of the great king Nebuchadnezzar, but had not had time to read further. He was intrigued to discover what Daniel had done to attract royal attention so many years before.

The scrolls had been returned to their proper places, so the appropriate one was easy to find. Alone once again in the library, he read how Daniel, also known as Belteshazzar, and three other Jewish captives of noble birth had been selected for training in the royal household. He read that Daniel and his friends had refused to eat the royal food or drink the palace wine, but insisted on a diet of vegetables and water in obedience to their god. This had been regarded with great suspicion, but allowed for a trial period of ten days, after which the health of the four Jews would be reassessed. They passed the test. At the end of their training, Nebuchadnezzar himself had interviewed the four youths and found them to excel in all matters of wisdom and understanding. Daniel was noted as the most excellent of the group.

The dawn was brightening, and with it Darius' mood. There was something about this Daniel and his god...

What Darius most hated about religion was the wasteful, domineering show that lured people into its web. But Daniel's faith was as understated as it was unswervingly honest.

Darius hurried out of the library, seized by a sudden urge to visit the lions' den. The few servants who were beginning to move around the palace stepped silently out of his way. Darius ran down into the basement and along the stone tunnel. He knelt, peering through the barred opening into the silent darkness of the lions' enclosure. His heart was pounding with the crazy hope kindled in him as he'd read about Daniel's youth.

'Daniel!' he called out. 'Daniel, servant of the one true God... has your God rescued you from the lions?'

He heard movement below him and could just make out a shifting shadow in the darkness.

'Is that you, Daniel?'

Darius could hardly believe that he was saying it. Yet, at that moment, the question made utter sense.

'Yes, your majesty. My God sent an angel to shut the lions' mouths. They have not hurt me.'

Darius' crazy hope exploded within him.

'Don't go away!' he told Daniel. A stupid thing to say!

Darius ran back along the tunnel and into his palace. He called to the first servant he saw, telling him to bring a rope, and some men to move the sealed stone. He also sent the duty commander of the Imperial Guard to fetch Buchnachaz and Cyrazzar.

Soon the gloomy dungeon was bright with torchlight. This time Darius gave the orders. Bewildered servants and soldiers pulled carefully on a new rope and Daniel was lifted out of the den.

There was not a scratch on him.

The emperor and the Jew stood looking at each other awkwardly. Darius did not know what to say. Deep inside, he felt like a child again – innocent and free.

Daniel said calmly, 'If you will excuse me, your majesty, I believe the sun is rising outside the palace and it is my custom to pray at this time.'

Darius dismissed Daniel with a rueful smile and a nod of his head.

One of the servants asked, 'Your majesty, would you like us to place the stone back over the opening?'

'No,' the king replied firmly. 'The lions must be hungry. I intend to serve them a lavish breakfast.'

FAMILY POLITICS

I T WAS NOT the rapturous welcome home Joseph had dreamed about. He had played this moment through his imagination so many times and each fantasy, in different ways, had featured running children, fond embraces and – the part that Joseph most longed for – sincere apologies. Instead, at the critical moment when the two dusty travellers came in view of Bethlehem's whitewashed walls and flat roofs, the ancient Jewish town carried on its own business with blank disinterest.

Joseph and his heavily pregnant fiancée, Mary, had completed the gruelling day-long climb through the heart of the wilderness and up into the mountains; the end of a one hundred and fifty mile trek, with Mary in the ninth month of her pregnancy – but who cared?

No one.

They should never have undertaken such a journey so near to the child's birth. But they had no choice. Roman laws might be open for debate in the marble courtyards of Rome, but in the occupied territories at the edge of the empire you did what you were told. Joseph had to register for the Roman census in his home town. Mary, as his legally contracted fiancée, had to go with him. They had to do it during the designated month. And that was that. If a young woman had to walk so far in such a condition, Rome did not care. And neither, it seemed, did Bethlehem.

Joseph paused within view of his childhood home. He was still hoping that his dreams might yet come true… that his ageing aunt Ruth might rush out to greet him. He paused to contemplate the bittersweet memories the familiar sight sent fluttering round his mind. He paused to consider, even at this final stage of their journey, turning round and walking all the way back to Nazareth.

Two things made him stay. The first was that Mary would need family support when the time came for her baby to be born, and they could never make it back to Nazareth in time. Joseph's family was their only choice. The second reason was an ancient and largely forgotten prophecy that a new king would one day emerge from the family of King David – greatest of all the Jewish kings – and that this king would be born in David's home town, Bethlehem. There were few people who cared for such ancient promises, but most of those were members of Joseph's family. Because Joseph's family, five hundred years on, were direct descendants of the Jewish kings.

So Joseph couldn't turn back. Mary's baby was important; he had been told so in a dream by an angel from God. If his family's favourite prophecy was to be fulfilled, Joseph would have to walk into the town and face Aunt Ruth.

Still he did not move.

Mary gave up waiting. Her swollen ankles, aching back and pounding heart drove her exhausted body into the shade of a leafy fig tree. She did not know what her loyal and loving husband-to-be was struggling with; he had not told her.

Joseph wandered over to a bored-looking young shepherd who was standing nearby, surrounded by sheep and goats.

'Do you know a woman called Ruth, daughter of ... ?' Joseph asked.

'Who doesn't?'

Joseph had nursed a fantasy that his aunt might have mellowed with age. Apparently she hadn't.

'You know her?' the shepherd asked, with only a hint of interest.

'My father's sister. Does she still live in Well Lane?' Joseph asked.

'You not from round here?'

A wry smile came to Joseph's face. Aunt Ruth had wanted Joseph to be a shepherd, but he chose to be a carpenter instead. According to social convention – in particular, Aunt Ruth's social convention – shepherds ranked above carpenters in the pecking order. Joseph's smile did not last long. A painful memory washed it away: it was Aunt Ruth's response to having a carpenter in her family that had driven Joseph as far away from Bethlehem as he dared travel.

'I need to ask Ruth for accommodation,' Joseph explained to the shepherd. 'We're here for the census.'

The shepherd routinely cast an eye across his flock, making sure they were all accounted for. Then he said, 'Luckily for you, they've just built a guest room on the roof. I think they're the only ones in that street with a guest room, so you'll spot the house straight away.'

Joseph made his way back to Mary, making a mental list of all the things he had yet to tell her about Aunt Ruth and the rest of his family in Bethlehem. The ghosts of his youth rose up from their uneasy rest: the clear reluctance with which Aunt Ruth had taken Joseph into her home when his parents died; her jealous protection of her own children in the presence of her slightly older nephew; his uncle's bitter criticism of his decision to be a carpenter; the screaming rows that finally drove Joseph to leave home and seek an apprenticeship in the far north. He had neither seen nor contacted Ruth since the day he left and now he was relying on her to accommodate him and his heavily pregnant fiancée. He knew that Aunt Ruth would look after them. Social custom demanded it. And Ruth was very keen on social custom. But that didn't mean it would be easy.

Joseph gently pulled Mary to her filthy feet. As they plodded wearily into the small town, he distracted her and himself with happier stories from his childhood from before his parents died.

'This is where we…'

'You see that house? That's where I…'

'One summer, when I was about nine…'

Mary laughed. It was a rare treat to hear about her future husband's past.

They came to the town's well – supposedly dug by King David himself – turned into a narrow, curving street and looked for the house with a new room constructed on its flat roof. It wasn't hard to find. It was the house with no fewer than five donkeys tied up outside. It was the house with a vast array of multicoloured washing hanging in the warm evening breeze. It was the house from which came all the shouting and bickering that filled the street.

Mary didn't care. It was family. It was the end of a tortuous journey. She was more than happy to trade a little family friction for a comfortable chair and a bowl of warm water for her blistered feet.

Joseph, though, suddenly felt sick. Memories of childhood fun vanished, replaced by the sound of half-familiar voices exchanging familiar insults. That was why he had left Bethlehem.

Had he been alone, Joseph would have turned around at that very moment and joined the shepherd who, no doubt, slept on the hillside every night. But he could not do that to Mary; she needed shelter in the home that he found so unbearable. Those final few yards seemed more daunting than any of the miles they had already travelled. Yet, it was a relief to stop. It was a relief for Joseph to put down the heavy pack. It was a relief for Mary to lean her back against the cool, smooth wall. But it was with a trembling hand that Joseph knocked on the door.

The yelling stopped. The door swung open. A sour-faced woman filled the doorway. 'Oh, it's you!' she snorted, out of breath from all her screaming. 'We thought you might be along sooner or later.'

'It is a privilege, Aunt Ruth, to be a guest in your home.' Joseph repeated the traditional greeting of a traveller claiming his right to hospitality from his relations.

'You can cut that nonsense,' Aunt Ruth retorted. 'I'm sure we can fit you in somehow, but I can't think where.' Her eyes settled on Mary. 'Is she with you?'

'Aunt Ruth, this is Mary. She is my fiancée.'

'Wife more like!' Ruth responded, looking at Mary's fully rounded belly.

'We are not yet married,' Joseph explained with determined politeness.

'You could have fooled me.' Ruth looked Joseph coldly in the eye. 'I suppose you didn't want us at your wedding. And I don't imagine you could afford to entertain your own family, being only a … what is it you do for a living?'

'I'm a carpenter.' Joseph fought to restrain his rising anger. 'You will all be invited to our wedding, of course. But we will not be married until after Mary's baby has been born.'

'Do you want your child to be born a …' Then she stopped, her eyes widening with realisation. 'Oh, I understand. *Mary's baby*. So you're taking on second-hand goods are you, Joseph? Why does that not surprise me?'

Aunt Ruth turned her attention to Mary, her tone of voice switching effortlessly from bitter sarcasm to silky charm. 'Come in, my dear. We can't have you standing on the doorstep, in your condition.'

Then she raised her voice to a practised screech: 'MIRIAM!'

Then back to self-conscious kindness: 'Sit yourself down, dear. Miriam will look after you.'

Then a second piercing yell: 'MIRIAM!'

'Yes, Mother?'

'Look after Joseph's young lady for me. She needs her feet washed, a drink and something to eat.'

'But, Mother!'

'DO IT!'

Miriam, who was a little older than Mary, shrivelled at her mother's command. She grabbed Mary by the arm and hurried her past a pile of rolled-up sleeping mats to the far corner of the house.

Aunt Ruth, re-attaching her gaze to the pale-faced Joseph, stepped out into the street, closing the door behind her. 'Right, Joseph, if you expect me to provide hospitality for your fiancée, I expect to be told the whole story.'

'It's rather complicated.'

'I don't doubt it.'

'The thing is…'

'That door does not open again until you've told me everything.'

'Aunt Ruth!'

'Everything.'

'Let me put it this way… The child is not mine.'

'I'd worked that out for myself.' Ruth's dislike for Joseph coloured her every word.

Joseph's patience began to buckle. 'Please give me a chance, Ruth. I will try to explain. It's just…'

'I am giving you a chance, Joseph. But just the one. I'm very busy. You're not the first member of the family to descend on me since Emperor whatever-his-name-is decided to squeeze some more money out of us.'

Joseph really did not want to tell the whole truth to his aunt. He himself had struggled to come to terms with Mary's story even though he loved her dearly. There seemed little chance of his aunt believing a single word of it.

He attempted a half-truth. 'The baby's father has asked me to adopt the child and bring him up as my own.'

'An unlikely story, but I'm listening.'

Joseph took in a slow breath. He knew that Ruth would squeeze every detail out of him. 'Mary and I were already engaged when …'

'You weakling! Was it for the money? If that's your problem, your uncle and I would help you – if you aren't too proud to ask.'

'It has nothing at all to do with money.' Joseph could hardly contain his anger. He spoke rapidly. 'I was going to break off the engagement, I was going to protect our family's name, but a messenger from the child's father told me to go ahead and marry Mary as planned. He told me that the father was…'

'A messenger?' Aunt Ruth squawked with disbelief. 'Couldn't the man who did this to your fiancée have the decency to visit you himself?'

'No… he couldn't,' Joseph mumbled. He felt like a naughty child. He felt sick. How could he tell this woman the truth? It was too extreme, too bizarre, too wonderful.

Ruth was impatient. 'Is he dead?'

Joseph could not restrain a small snort of laughter at the absurdity of Ruth's question. This irate woman had no inkling that when Joseph talked about the father of Mary's child, he was talking about God.

'Ruth, could we discuss this somewhere more private?'

'This is as private as it gets, Joseph. Your Uncle Dan and his wife and their seven children, and your Uncle Eliab with his wife and four little ones, along with all my own children and grandchildren – with the exception of Jesse, my eldest, and Michal, who still live in the town – have all come to stay in my house because of Governor Quirinius' damned census.'

She was shouting. A young couple looked across the road at her as they passed. Joseph felt a pang of pity for his proud aunt, even though she was carrying out her cultural obligations with so little grace.

'Out here in the street will be fine,' he said calmly. Then he guided Aunt Ruth to a sun-bleached wooden bench surrounded by drying laundry. His cousins' younger children were playing 'Romans and Zealots' with wooden swords a short distance away, but the damp linen created an illusion of privacy.

'Ruth,' Joseph began cautiously. 'You have always been very proud of our family's ancestry.'

She gave a dignified nod. Joseph knew he was on the right track.

'You were the one who told me that God's Messiah was going to come from our family.'

She nodded again.

Then Joseph added self-mockingly, 'You also told me that it certainly wasn't going to be me.'

'Well, I was right, wasn't I? The Messiah – when he comes – will come from Bethlehem, not from Nazareth or wherever it is you live now.'

She knew she was pressing on an old wound, but Joseph mastered his emotions.

'That is right,' he conceded. 'The Messiah will be born in this town, in David's town.' He had Aunt Ruth's attention now, he knew it. This was her favourite subject. She could bore anyone with a precise recitation of her family tree, through King David all the way back to Abraham (or even to Adam and Eve if the listener lacked the courage to stop her).

'Ruth,' Joseph continued, 'the Messiah is going to be born in this house, in your house, this month.' He gave her time to absorb this information. 'The ancient prophecy you have talked about and dreamed of all your life is about to be fulfilled. And you will see it with your own eyes.'

The old woman was silenced. She stared at her nephew with shock and disbelief. She had always harboured a certain resentment against Joseph, because he was the eldest son of her elder brother. If she only knew it, she had driven him away from Bethlehem in order that her own son would be at the front of the queue should God decide that the time had come for Israel's promised saviour to emerge. She looked into Joseph's wise, pained and anxious eyes with equal measures of delight and jealousy.

Joseph continued, 'The father of Mary's child, Ruth, is God. Her child is the Messiah. And God has asked me to be stepfather to the boy.'

Aunt Ruth's remarkable talent for a withering riposte was defeated. Joseph looked steadily into her startled eyes. The outrageous facts of his situation still stretched his own ability to be amazed; he could not imagine how they might sound to Aunt Ruth. When he spoke again, it was gently.

'The messenger I mentioned was an …'

Her eyes were suddenly wide. 'You've seen an angel?'

Three small boys came charging through the drying sheets, wooden swords in hands. 'Nanna, Nanna, you're Emperor Augustus and we're going to kill you.'

Nanna was too shocked to meet this interruption with her usual acidity. Her eyes did not leave Joseph's; she left her grandsons to wander uncertainly away, surprised by the lack of reaction.

'I didn't actually see an angel,' Joseph explained modestly. 'It was more of a dream.' He noted the disappointment in his aunt's eyes. 'But Mary did. She was visited by angel Gabriel.' He knew that would impress the old lady.

There was a long silence while his aunt's mind visited a thousand fondly held fantasies. Joseph, meanwhile, revisited every word that had been said since he arrived in Bethlehem. Had he been right to tell Ruth? He wasn't sure. She was his closest living relative. But she was not renowned for her discretion. He and Mary had been meticulous in keeping God's secret. The only other person who knew the whole story was Mary's elderly aunt Elizabeth. But they were not the ones who had told Elizabeth; God had.

Eventually Aunt Ruth let out a long sigh. Joseph knew that sigh. It meant that she had finished her deliberations. She blinked several times, looked at Joseph, pulled a rather false smile and announced, 'You still can't have the guest room.'

TWO WEEKS LATER

The house was ridiculously full. Each night, the floor of the downstairs room was covered with blanket-wrapped bodies. Mary was obliged to sleep near the door along with the youngest children, owing to her need to take frequent trips outside during the night. Aunt Ruth and the rest of the older generation had taken the privilege of seniority and were sharing the guest room on the roof. No one was sleeping well. Everyone was irritable.

It was not easy for Joseph to find work. Ruth's was not the only overcrowded household in the town. The census had swollen Bethlehem beyond capacity and there were more carpenters than there were jobs at a time when no one was contemplating improvements to their homes.

Things were no easier for Mary. Aunt Ruth maintained the secrecy of the true circumstances of Mary's pregnancy, so the rest of the family believed that Mary was, at best, a former prostitute Joseph had taken it on himself to rescue. They took their lead from Ruth's somewhat harsh behaviour towards the young woman.

Mary and Joseph kept mostly to themselves. Mary filled much of her time rehearsing her anxieties about the forthcoming birth. Who would help her through the labour? Back home in Nazareth, babies were delivered by the married women of the village, so she had never been included. She knew very little about what to expect. When she and Joseph had set off for Bethlehem, her mother had said, 'Don't worry, Mary. Joseph's family will look after you.'

But would they?

Where would the child sleep? If he was born before the family were called to register for the census, the floor was so crowded it would not be safe to have a newborn at her side. He could be crushed. Joseph was still hoping that Ruth would let them have the guest room, but he had not yet dared raise the matter with his aunt. Mary felt it was quite possible that Aunt Ruth would throw them out of the house as soon as the baby was born.

Inevitably, the time came. Mary's labour began in the early part of the night.

She lay wide-eyed as her pains grew in frequency and intensity. That day had been terrible, with Ruth repeatedly accusing her of not helping. Hurtful names had been thrown at her during the afternoon, which echoed in Mary's thoughts as she faced the lonely hours of the night.

When she was no longer able to manage the pain in silence, Mary waddled out into the warm night air, alone.

Some while later Joseph noted that his fiancée's small space on the communal floor was vacant. He slipped out and found Mary in the street, crouching low with her back resting against the wall. She was breathing heavily and tears flowed freely down her cheeks. He stared at her in blank terror. Mary knew little of the mysteries of childbirth; Joseph knew far less. He gripped her hand and released his own long-constrained tears.

'I don't know what to do,' he sobbed.

Mary panted in and out in rushed, fearful breaths. Her pains passed for a while and as she released her vice-like grip on Joseph's hand, she said weakly, 'We need help.'

'I'll get Ruth,' Joseph conceded.

Ruth was fantastic. She quietly roused the other four mothers in the household and soon had them rushing round at her command. Whatever animosities the women held against Mary were given no chance for expression as Ruth coordinated the safe arrival of God's Messiah. Joseph was kept at a distance, always given another task to prevent him from entering the secret circle of motherhood and childbirth. He lit a fire. He boiled water. He fetched lamps. He tore up strips of cloth. He made drinks. He did not mind; it was better than doing nothing.

It was all over remarkably quickly. In a blur of agony, with Ruth never leaving her side, Mary gave that final, exhausted squeeze which brought her baby son into the life-sustaining air. He was then delivered, wet and warm, softly crying and blindly nuzzling, to her breast. The pains of the previous hours were instantly forgotten, as were the insults of recent days. While Joseph's cousins continued to attend to her, Mary looked with speechless amazement into her child's eyes.

'Will he be called Joseph?' Ruth asked. The hint of uncertainty in her voice betrayed her continuing dislike of her eldest nephew. 'I think David would be more appropriate.'

Mary replied quietly, without breaking from her son's infant gaze, 'He is called Jesus.'

There was an uncomfortable silence, into which Ruth added a disappointed, 'Oh!'

Mary was familiar with the petty jealousies that arise in families over the names of babies. She also knew that this child had been given his name by Gabriel, and that the angel, she assumed, had received his instructions from God.

'His name is Jesus,' confirmed Joseph.

'God save us,' muttered Miriam, continuing to clean Mary's legs with warm, damp cloths.

'God save us, indeed,' Ruth added pointedly, sweeping aside her daughter's spitefulness.

When all was clean and the tiny child wrapped in brightly coloured strips of soft, clean cloth, Ruth sent everyone to their beds.

'Where will Jesus sleep?' Mary asked, clutching her newborn son protectively to her chest.

The women all turned to look at her with questioning surprise. 'With you, of course,' Ruth replied.

'It's too crowded,' Mary insisted, struggling to hold back a torrent of tears. 'There's barely room for Joseph and me. It would only take someone to roll in the wrong direction and...'

'Joseph can sleep outside,' Ruth suggested harshly.

It was too much. Mary's resolve gave way; her tears flowed. Ruth's daughter-in-law Sarah came to her defence.

'I'm not sure that Joseph sleeping outside would make much difference, Mother. We would all just spread out a little and there would still be a danger of someone rolling onto the little one.'

All eyes looked at Ruth. Ruth pursed her lips as she considered various possibilities.

'There – that will do the job!' She pointed outside towards the donkeys munching on hay from a box fixed to the wall.

Mary and Joseph looked up in horror.

'Don't just stand there!' she barked at Joseph. 'Lift it off the wall.'

Joseph moved towards the wall in a daze. He pushed the donkeys out of the way and took the weight of the haybox on his carpenter's arms. It rose easily off a wooden bracket. Despite the emotional confusion of the night, he could not help a moment's admiration for the simple but effective design.

'There's another bracket here,' Ruth explained, 'for when we bring the animals inside in the winter.'

Joseph carried the box inside. It fitted firmly onto a bracket beside the door, just above the place where Mary slept each night. He pushed some fresh soft hay down into the box to create a safe bed for their child.

The women dispersed to their beds, a good night's work completed and all achieved without disturbing any of the husbands or children. Mary carefully placed her tiny son in the sanctuary of the wall-mounted manger and rested her own fatigued body on the narrow mat beneath it.

Joseph lay awake, struggling to make sense of the past nine months: angels and announcements; jealousies and journeys; families, fears – and a newborn child laid in a haybox because there was no other space in the house.

These thoughts swirled aimlessly round his mind until they were displaced by voices – excited voices – shouting their way up the street, babbling some nonsense about angels and sheep. A crazy dream?

Then, 'Will you great buffoons shut up and go away? We've been up all night helping the birth of a baby.' It was Ruth's voice from the guest room on the roof.

The word 'baby' brought an excited cheer from the revellers.

'And have you put it in a manger, this baby?' a rustic voice enquired.

'As it happens, we have,' Aunt Ruth replied, her voice prim.

The shepherds cheered again.

It wasn't a dream. Joseph threw aside his blanket and hurried to greet the visitors.

15 MONTHS LATER

The visit of the shepherds had clarified the whole situation for Ruth. If God was even sending his messengers to common shepherds, then he was certainly doing something significant.

Once the family had been called to register for the Roman census and the other visitors had returned to their own homes, Joseph, Mary and Jesus were promoted to the upstairs guest room. The old woman could not have been more accommodating. She reminded Joseph repeatedly that it would be best if they waited until the child was older before attempting the long journey back north. Just as often, she expressed her heartfelt opinion that Jesus really should be brought up in Bethlehem, just as his ancestor King David had been.

Ruth also worked hard to persuade her friends and neighbours that they too should have guest rooms built on their roofs, ready for the next imperial stupidity. And always, in her next breath, she recommended Joseph's skills as a carpenter and general builder.

So the family stayed. Mary and Joseph were married. Jesus grew. He smiled his first smile, cut his first tooth, spoke his first words and walked his first steps – all within the walls of Great-Aunt Ruth's home and under her watchful gaze. Ruth herself continued to shout, nag, boast and yell. But it was noticed that whenever her sharp tongue was directed at Mary or Jesus, she was always uncharacteristically quick with an apology. She had no desire to hurry the day when Joseph built his own home in the town and she was no longer housing the long-promised Messiah.

They arrived early one evening. Joseph had not yet returned from work. Mary was upstairs, preparing Jesus for bed. Ruth was cooking. They heard the sound of horses' hooves in the street. Everyone in the street ran to their doorways and windows to see what excitement the unfamiliar noise was bringing.

The horses slowed from a canter to a trot and then to a walk.

'Mummy, Mummy, look!' Jesus shouted from the top of the stairs.

There were four wealthy men accompanied by as many servants and two or three armed guards. The masters – clearly identified by their richly woven clothes – were intently studying the skyline behind the houses. When they reached the steps that led to the half-naked Jesus, they stopped and dismounted. Mary rushed out of the guest room and swept her son into her arms.

'We have come from King Herod.' The voice was strongly accented.

Ruth stepped forward and bowed. 'How can I help you, sir?'

'We are looking for the child who has been born to be a king to the Jews,' the stranger said.

The foreign visitor followed her automatic gaze and began to climb the stairs.

He stopped halfway. 'It is as you expected,' he called to one of his companions. 'The star must have appeared at the time of the child's conception.' He turned his attention upwards, to Mary. 'How old is the boy, my lady? If our calculations are correct, and this is indeed the child, he will be one year and three moons.'

'He is,' Mary said calmly. Of all the fascinated faces looking on, hers was the least surprised. 'Please come up.'

Ruth butted in. 'Gentlemen, why don't you come into our main room? There will be more space. I have already prepared a meal. Please accept my humble hospitality.'

The man looked at Mary. His enquiring face and upturned hands invited her to choose which room they should meet in.

'We'll come down,' she said.

While Ruth busied herself with the challenge of feeding so many mouths, Mary ushered the four men and their entourage inside.

The strangers told their story. They worshipped the Great Spirit who created the heavens, studying the stars in order to know their God better. They had seen a particular configuration of stars in the eastern sky which informed them of a new king, born in Judea, where the Creator Spirit was also worshipped. This king, they believed, would bring the knowledge of God to the whole world. They had travelled westward for many months and scoured Jerusalem for information about the child, but without joy. Then King Herod, hearing of their enquiries, had arranged a secret meeting with them. He had directed their search to the ancient town of Bethlehem. Then, after so many months and so many miles, they had seen the same star again – directly over Bethlehem.

Mary, in turn, told her story: how an angel from God visited her and told her that she would have a son without the need for a human father because the child would be the Son of God himself.

The men listened with great interest, occasionally conferring among themselves in their own language or asking for further clarification on particular details.

Jesus, all this time, crawled among them all ... fiddling with new and shining things, crying when he banged his head, and repeatedly saying, 'What's this?' whenever he noticed something else he had never seen before.

Ruth served supper. Afterwards each of the four visitors in turn pulled the sleepy toddler up onto their laps and studied him intently. They held his hands, gazed into his dark eyes, touched his soft cheeks, always with a gentleness that encouraged the child's trust. And each, in his own way, ended this investigation by murmuring prayers over Jesus.

Ruth scowled at this peculiar behaviour, but Mary watched carefully, reassuring Jesus with smiles whenever he looked to her.

A servant was sent outside to fetch something from the masters' luggage. Leather bags were brought in and opened. First, each visitor presented Jesus with a purse filled with pure gold. Ruth's eyes were wide with amazement.

Next a small sack of brown granules was placed on Jesus' lap and carefully opened. Ruth could not restrain a gasp. She had never seen so much frankincense or traveller's gold as it was called – lighter and more valuable than real gold – even at the Temple market in Jerusalem. The men playfully encouraged Jesus to smell the granules of pungent resin. He screwed up his nose and turned to his mother's embrace.

The men laughed, carefully tied up the sack, and placed it – all of it – on the floor beside the four small purses of gold.

'I expect you will not like this much more, little king,' the spokesman of the four visitors suggested, handing Jesus another linen sack, much like the first. This, too, was opened. It contained granules of darker dried resin – myrrh, just as rare and just as valuable as frankincense. Again, Jesus was encouraged to feel and smell the valuable gift before the sack was tied and placed carefully on the floor.

The man who seemed to be the leader of these strange visitors then took a firm hold of Mary's hand. Their attention had been devoted to Jesus for such a long time that this shift of emphasis brought with it an atmosphere of serious intensity. At that moment Joseph appeared in the doorway. The men had their backs to him, and Mary's attention was firmly held. Only Jesus saw him.

'These things will provide for you and your son…' the leader of the Magi told the young mother. Then he added solemnly, '… wherever you go.' His companions nodded knowingly.

Ruth looked anxiously from the old man's face to the young woman's. She had worked so hard to keep Mary and Joseph in Bethlehem. Were they now being encouraged to leave?

The man's attention remained fixed on Mary. He repeated, '… wherever you go.' Then added, 'God will go with you,' as he released Mary's hand.

The strange visitors departed soon afterwards. They declined Ruth's offer of accommodation, saying that they had to return to King Herod first thing in the morning.

Joseph gathered up the amazing gifts and Mary carried her sleepy son up to his small bed. Ruth gave Jesus a gentle kiss on the head. It was the last time she would ever see the boy.

Joseph woke, sweating with fear. It had happened again, but this time it was terrifying. The first time an angel appeared in his dreams, he had woken to a feeling of deep peace. This time, however, he woke damp with sweat, adrenalin pumping through his veins. His dream had been of brutal soldiers, screaming mothers, bloody swords… then little boys, more little boys… and then numb disbelieving grief.

The angel – the same angel he had dreamed before – had chased him through every harrowing scene, screaming after him, 'Get out! Go! Don't come back! Not until I tell you! Go! GO! Go to Egypt!'

The next morning Ruth found the guest room empty. There was a small pile of gold on the table, and a little bowl filled with frankincense. The note read: 'For Ruth, from Joseph. The frankincense is in appreciation for your hospitality for the past year and more. The gold is in payment for your youngest donkey, which we have taken. The angel appeared to me again in a dream warning us to flee to Egypt. We have gone.'

Within a week, King Herod's private army had slaughtered every boy under the age of two in Bethlehem.

An impossible request

'THAT'S JUST STUPID,' James snapped.

'It's what he said,' Philip replied defensively. His mind squirmed. If he were honest about his own feelings he would have agreed with James. It was stupid. But he couldn't allow himself to think that way.

'Perhaps I misheard him,' he volunteered. But he knew he hadn't.

'There's no way we can feed all these people,' James insisted. 'There must be thousands of them.'

Philip said nothing. There *were* thousands of them.

Philip and James had had a trying day. They had had a trying month. They had returned the previous evening from a month-long tour. They were used to touring: walking from village to village, telling stories in marketplaces, debating in synagogues, sleeping in strange beds, following their rabbi. But this last tour had been different: same routine, but without the rabbi – just the two of them. On this tour, it was Philip and James who had to decide which village to visit next; Philip and James had to tell the stories; Philip and James had to deal with the awkward questions from suspicious Pharisees. It had been a very different tour indeed.

Now, back home, all they wanted was some rest and to return to their old familiar routines. But they were woken early – ridiculously early – by a group of total strangers milling around outside James' house, looking for Jesus.

Philip tried to be polite to the visitors, though his patience was certainly tested. James, typically, did not even try to be polite. He told them, with a fisherman's bluntness, exactly what he thought about being woken up so early. His angry outburst brought a predictable backlash: 'You call yourself religious, and you use language like that?'

James demonstrated an even broader repertoire of expletives which, although quite common among the Galilean fishing fleet, were nothing short of scandalous on the lips of a disciple of the rabbi-of-the-moment Jesus, the former builder from Nazareth.

The strangers were duly shocked. They had walked through the night to hear comforting parables and see exciting miracles, not be sworn at by a foul-mouthed fisherman. And James' tongue, once set loose, was not easily restrained. Philip did try, but without success. James announced, 'I'm quite sure that Jesus himself employed a few colourful phrases on the building sites around Nazareth.'

At that moment, Jesus himself emerged from his makeshift bed on the floor in a corner of James' room. And, unrecognised by those at the door – possibly because of the state of his hair – he gently but firmly pulled James inside, closed the door on the disgruntled strangers, and bolted it.

'We need to go somewhere quiet and get some rest,' he yawned.

A few minutes later, Jesus was the first to climb out through the back window of James' house. James followed, and the two of them guided Philip's larger and less agile frame gently to the ground. They could hear numerous expressions of indignant confusion coming from the narrow street at the front of the house. So, silently and bending low behind successive stone walls, rabbi and disciples made their way towards Andrew's house at the far end of the village, where they had arranged to meet for breakfast. Philip could not remember when he last played such a game of cat and mouse; probably when his two children were young. His body was not built for such activities. James, on the other hand, was thoroughly enjoying himself.

The three of them darted and scurried to the far side of the village. They made it to the relative safety of an overgrown olive orchard that separated Andrew's home from the rest of Capernaum. Hidden from sight by the overgrowth, they could hear muddled fragments of conversation coming from the road. There were a lot more strangers around, all looking for Jesus.

Jesus stopped and listened. He leaned back uncertainly against an ancient olive tree, his eyes tight closed; indecision was written across his face. Should he meet the needs of those who had walked many miles to hear him teaching about God? Or should he see to the needs of his exhausted disciples, who had just returned from their first 'solo' tour?

James had quickly forgotten his anger at being woken and was simply enjoying the adventure. Philip, aware of his rabbi's dilemma, hovered uneasily beside Jesus, and let out a long sigh. After a month of travelling with James, he knew a lot about making difficult decisions. But he had always assumed that the right course of action came naturally to Jesus. Jesus looked at him, his lips pressed tightly together. Apparently not.

This was unsettling. James might enjoy climbing out of windows in the early hours of the morning, but Philip liked life to be more predictable. His expression communicated to Jesus, 'Don't look to me for inspiration.'

The rabbi took in a long, deep breath, and jumped forwards, leading the way onwards through the olive grove, over a high wall (Philip once again requiring assistance), and round to the back of Andrew's home.

The narrow back door was firmly bolted; they heard the noise of a gathering crowd at the front of the house. Jesus' knocking was ignored. Evidently the rest of Jesus' disciples had retreated from the siege.

'You're the victims of your own success,' Jesus commented as he, Philip and James regained their breath in the relative safety of Andrew's back yard.

'What success?' James asked.

'All those people,' Jesus was still struggling for breath, 'were so impressed by your teaching that they've come to hear more.'

Philip wasn't convinced. 'They're looking for you, not us.'

'Yes,' Jesus agreed. 'But they wouldn't be looking for me, if it wasn't for you.'

James was spitting on his fingers, trying to clean off a graze on his knee. 'Remind me not to do so well next time,' he observed. 'Anyway, I'm hungry.'

Jesus began to pile empty fish baskets against the wall under a rear window high up. He climbed up, and looked in at the ten tired, hungry men inside.

'What happened to breakfast?' he asked cheerily. Ten heads spun round to see their rabbi's smiling face framed in the small, square window.

'It's out there,' Peter said grumpily, indicating the walled yard full of unwanted visitors at the front of his brother's house. 'Andrew just got it all laid out, when that lot arrived.'

The first part of their plan – to sneak out the back way and get down to the lake shore without being seen – was successful. But their attempt to crowd into and launch Peter and James' fishing boats without being noticed, failed miserably. As they rowed the overloaded vessels round the edge of the lake, the excited crowd tracked their progress along the shore. Unless Jesus and his disciples opted for spending the entire day on the water crammed into two small fishing boats, there was no chance of escape.

Jesus came to a decision. He'd been watching the people for nearly an hour as they darted through the orchards and plantations along the lakeside. His attention was stretched between the tales of his disciples' first preaching tour, and the shouts of their pursuers. Where the trees and shrubs ended, giving way to a grass-covered hillside, Jesus' attention was drawn to the familiar sight of a shepherd standing near the shore, his wooden staff slung across his shoulders, idly watching the tatty assortment of sheep and goats around him.

Jesus said, 'They are like sheep without a shepherd.'

The disciples looked at their rabbi, wondering what he meant. Philip followed Jesus' gaze towards the invading mass who had already cost him his lie-in and his breakfast. He didn't feel any sympathy for them.

'Pull ashore over there,' said Jesus. 'We all have some teaching to do.'

Philip and James were astounded that by the time they'd pulled the boat out of the water, hundreds of people had appeared on the hillside – with more arriving every minute.

Jesus climbed part way up the grassy hill and sat down to teach. The crowd flocked around, jostling for a view of the unconventional rabbi. For the rest of the morning, through the heat of the day and well into the afternoon, the people pressed around to listen to his stories of sheep and fishing nets, fruit trees and wheat crops. Every now and then, Jesus would dismiss those at the front of the crowd to the back, and start all over again with a fresh batch of listeners.

All hope of rest long abandoned, Jesus instructed his disciples to spread out in pairs around the back of the crowd, to tell his stories for those who were still waiting for their chance to listen to Jesus himself. Philip and James sat by the shore, where they could keep a watchful eye on James' precious boat. They fell quickly into the routine of the past few weeks: telling stories, answering questions, trying their best to say what they thought Jesus would say, but never quite feeling confident about it. The people listened, occasionally glancing up the slope to see if Jesus was ready for a new audience.

Throughout the day more and more families arrived. The only person to leave that remote pasture was the bewildered shepherd.

Philip and James took turns at retelling Jesus' most popular stories. At one point – while James was recounting the saga of two brothers, the younger of which travelled the world, lost everything, and returned to his father – Philip gazed at the familiar landscape framing the Sea of Galilee. It seemed remarkable that he should be sitting there teaching a large crowd of total strangers about God. Two years before he was a moderately successful farmer with a small, generally happy, family. He rarely entered the synagogue, never spoke in public, and only ever prayed when he had exhausted all other possibilities. He remembered he had done a lot of praying some years ago when his only daughter was dying. But God, as far as Philip could tell at the time, had not responded.

Philip had not gone running after Jesus, as James and Andrew had done. He'd had no time for Messiahs and talk of salvation. There was a farm to run and a family to feed. He had, of course, heard of Jesus; and he wasn't interested. Not until the day that Jesus came to him, just after the barley harvest.

'I'm looking for an honest man,' Jesus had said, as he helped Philip lift several sacks of barley husks into his small grain store.

'I try to be that,' Philip had replied, rather uncomfortable to find himself talking to a rabbi.

'Good,' Jesus had smiled. 'Come with me, then, and I'll teach you how to harvest men and women.'

And that had been it. Contrary to everything Philip had ever said or thought about rabbis and disciples and the ever-flourishing business of religion. He asked his son to mind the farm and went off with Jesus. He still couldn't quite believe it. But here he was, sitting on the grass, with at least three hundred people standing around him to hear him talk to them about God.

James' story had finished. It was Philip's turn. He chose Jesus' parable about a farmer whose rival sowed weeds among his barley crop.

The shadows were lengthening in front of them. Afternoon was turning rapidly to evening. Philip felt exhaustion creeping through his mind and body. He had not eaten all day – no one had – and it would soon be dark. He left James midway through a story and climbed the hill to speak to Jesus. These people needed to eat. As Philip puffed his rotund frame up the grassy slope, he chuckled at the thought that it fell to him to turn Jesus' mind from the business of heaven to more practical concerns.

'This is a remote place,' he reminded his young rabbi in a brief pause between stories, 'and it's getting late. Send the people away, so they can go to the villages and buy food for themselves.'

It was then that Jesus gave the instruction which threw Philip into a chaotic complex of uncertainty and self-doubt and James described as 'just stupid'.

Jesus looked up at Philip and, with characteristic charm, said, 'You give them something to eat.'

Philip felt quite faint at the suggestion. He knew well enough how much hard sweat and patience it took to produce enough food for even a small family. The prospect of feeding quite so many people hurled him far beyond the reach of his imagination. He stared at Jesus in disbelief. The rabbi smiled sympathetically and launched into another story, the one about a man who found a box of treasure buried in a field. Philip staggered, light-headed, back towards James, muttering to himself, 'It would have to be a flippin' big hoard of treasure to feed this lot!'

'Completely stupid!' James repeated. The two disciples abandoned their audience and retreated to the relative privacy of the shore to talk. 'There's no way we can feed so many people.'

'How many do you think there are?' Philip asked.

They looked hopelessly around them. There were certainly thousands. But how many thousands? And how much would so many people eat?

A woman's voice emerged above the chatter, 'I know you're hungry, but you'll just have to wait.'

Philip's mind raced with guilt. He spun round to identify his accuser. It was a young mother talking to a small boy. The comment was not addressed to Philip after all. He returned to his calculations.

The same voice rang out again, exasperated: 'I don't have anything you can eat!'

Philip felt he had been right to bring this problem to Jesus' attention. Only, he hadn't expected that he would be left to solve it. He tried to gain control of his feelings. He was a problem solver. Farming was a never-ending series of problems and solutions. In his experience, all problems had a solution, if only you could find it. He even believed that to be true in the case of his only daughter's desperate illness. He still blamed himself for not solving that particular problem. Jesus had simply set him another one – feeding thousands of people in the middle of nowhere when it was about to get dark. He just needed to work it out.

He began his calculations again. How much bread might one hungry person eat? How many hungry people were there? Soon he had introduced new sums. What were the relative prices of wheat and barley? What was the standard hourly wage for a baker?

Jesus had asked *him*, Philip reassured himself, because he was the kind of man who could make calculations like these. When he had finished pushing the numbers around his head, he concluded that it would require the equivalent of three hundred days' labour to provide a reasonable meal for the present crowd – far and away more money than he had in his small purse. He would need more cash… a lot more cash.

He asked James to climb on top of a nearby outcrop of rock to look for Judas. Judas kept the communal accounts for Jesus and his disciples when they travelled together. He would have more cash in his purse than Philip did.

Judas could not be seen. He was somewhere in the middle of that hill of people.

The sun was sinking. Time was against them. Philip and James set off in search of Judas.

'What are you looking for?'

The voice was Andrew's.

Philip explained: 'Jesus has asked us to feed all this lot.'

'What do you mean: feed?' Hunger and tiredness gave an impatient edge to Andrew's voice.

'Give them some bread, I assume,' Philip said, blankly.

The ludicrous nature of the task overwhelmed them. The three friends stared, defeated, at the restless ocean of humanity.

'What exactly did Jesus say?' James asked, not even attempting to hide his assumption that Philip must have made a mistake.

'I suggested that Jesus send the people into the villages to buy food,' Philip recounted. 'And he said, "You give them something to eat." I'm quite sure of it.' He had spotted the questioning look in James' eyes.

Andrew let a low whistle escape his lips. 'By my calculations, there are at least five thousand.' He set off resolutely up the hill, heading for Jesus.

Philip trotted after him, updating the tall fisherman with his financial assessment. And James followed. When the three of them had picked their way to Jesus they waited in a sullen row, like naughty children, for the unsettling conclusion to Jesus' story about five bridesmaids who missed a wedding because they were not ready when the bridegroom arrived.

Jesus turned to greet them. 'How are you getting on?' he asked cheerfully.

Their slumped shoulders said everything. Philip looked carefully into his rabbi's animated eyes. He had little doubt that Jesus knew what was going on in the farmer's head. They had been in similar situations before. On each occasion Philip had struggled to see how he would solve the problem facing him and on each occasion Jesus had urged him to bring God into his calculations. It was not an idea that came naturally to Philip. However he looked at it, the numbers remained the same. With or without God, bread still cost money… unless you made it yourself.

He spoke up. 'Thr…' He stopped himself, determined to be as optimistic as possible. 'Two hundred denarii should just about buy enough bread for everyone to have a bit, but I haven't a clue where we could buy it, so…'

Jesus looked amused. Clearly, then, he did not intend him to buy the bread. That was a relief, but it didn't help much. He had no alternative plan… unless Jesus meant him to bake the bread. No, that was even more ridiculous.

'How much bread do you have?' Jesus asked.

Philip reprimanded himself for not having thought of that. Why did he always count up what he did not have, rather than what he did have? Of course, someone was bound to have some food.

The three disciples left Jesus to continue with his teaching, splitting up to tour the whole hungry crowd, recruiting their colleagues as they went, to search for bread.

Philip's optimism did not last long. For a few moments he believed that anything was possible. For those brief moments he felt like a true follower of Jesus – like Peter and John. But some time before he arrived, empty-handed, at the agreed meeting place – James' boat – his hope had gone. Only Andrew had found any food. A young boy had given him five small flat barley rounds and two even smaller fish. Philip could have eaten the lot, including the little basket, and still been hungry.

The twelve stared hopelessly at the meagre offering. No one spoke. There was nothing worth saying.

Again they had to wait for Jesus to finish a story. He was talking about how a small amount of yeast silently makes a whole batch of bread dough rise. Philip was not amused to hear Jesus talking about bread, while he was holding the five small – disappointingly small – barley baps.

'Well done,' Jesus said when he turned to his disciples and saw the sorry offering. Philip was startled by the strength and integrity of Jesus' praise. It was the praise he might have expected if he had been standing there with a cart piled high with fresh bread.

Jesus held out his hands and Philip handed over the basket. For a moment, Jesus nestled the food in his lap, as if he was holding a priceless treasure. Then he looked up and prayed the same prayer of thanks that Philip had heard him pray a hundred times, whenever they ate together. As he prayed, Jesus broke each of the small bread rounds into two, just as he would at any meal.

Then, again entirely normally, Jesus handed half of each piece to nine of his disciples and gave the remaining half to the young girl sitting next to him. 'Break it up and pass it round,' he instructed.

His instruction would have been utterly sensible if there were no more than twenty of them needing a quick snack. In the circumstances, Philip found it hard to consider Jesus' instruction as anything other than a poor joke.

But Jesus was not joking. And Philip – for all his rational confusion – had learned to trust his unconventional teacher. He took a few steps towards the nearest group of people, invited them to sit down, broke his small piece of bread in half and handed it to a young boy.

'I'm sorry we haven't got much,' he said. 'But it's better than nothing.'

He then broke his remaining piece in half again and handed it to the boy's father. He was expecting complaints at the meanness of his portions but the young family was too busy eating.

It was some time before Philip realised that the chunks of bread he was distributing were not getting any smaller. When he had circumnavigated the whole group of about twenty-five people, he noticed that the small boy was still holding most of his quarter piece. 'It's yours,' Philip reassured him.

The boy mumbled something incomprehensible though a full mouth.

At that moment, James bounded recklessly over the small boy's head, landing in the middle of the family circle.

'Amazing!' he announced, flapping half a dried fish in front of Philip's nose.

'Look! Half a fish…' He darted around the same group of Galileans, tearing off chunks of salty fish for each of them, incautious with the portions. Quickly, James served every member of the group and was waving the remains, once again, under Philip's nose. 'See? Still half a fish!'

Philip began to understand how the little boy could still be holding most of his chunk of bread while also chomping on a large mouthful. He looked around. His colleagues were all dashing around, handing out chunks of bread and fish. The people sitting on the ground each had a piece of bread in one hand, a chunk of fish in the other, and a mouth full of one or other, if not both.

'Sorry, I couldn't manage it all,' an elderly woman apologised as she dropped a fragment of bread into the fish basket that Philip had brought from James' boat. Jesus had insisted that they clear up all the uneaten bread and fish abandoned as the day's bumper crowd finally dissolved, bellies full, into the night.

There was a lot to clear up. Each of Jesus' twelve disciples had a basket, and each of the baskets was mostly full.

Philip quietly made his way to the place where Jesus had gathered a small mound of leftovers.

'How did that happen?' he asked, as they both scooped the scraps into his basket.

The parable of Josiah and Titch

'Hey, Levi!'

'Titch! How are you?'

'I'm doing well. Wheeling and dealing as ever.'

Levi, the taller of the two men, nodded. It was a nod of understanding and acceptance, but not of approval. The old acquaintances stood in the crowded marketplace, causing everyone else to flow round them. The hubbub of commerce required them to shout at one another. But there they stood, Levi looking down, Titch looking up, both pleased to have met the other.

'I heard you quit the business, Levi.'

Another nod, this one more committed.

'So… who pays better than the Roman emperor?' Titch asked.

'I just quit.'

They were separated momentarily by a succession of small children racing between them. Levi smiled at them. Titch didn't.

Levi said, 'If we can find somewhere a bit quieter, I'll tell you about it.'

Titch knew the town well and led the way. Levi followed his former colleague across the market square and down a narrow alley lined with shabby whitewashed houses. They could have stopped anywhere in that street and leaned against someone's home, but Titch was looking for somewhere more comfortable.

The street broadened for a short distance where there was a small orchard on one side.

'This will do,' Levi suggested.

Titch walked on. He knew who the orchard belonged to; he would not be welcome under its shade. He walked purposefully on to the edge of town, until they had passed the last home.

'So Levi, my old friend, who or what has lured you away from the best paid job in the province? Surely you didn't give in to the moaners and whingers?'

Levi leaned against a boundary wall and breathed in the clear air.

'I've left the money business altogether. One morning I got up, walked out of my office and never went back.'

Titch bobbed his head from side to side as he drew together these fragments of information. 'That's what I heard,' he said. 'I just didn't believe it.'

'Well, it's true.'

'The rumour is, you got religion.'

'I wouldn't call it religion, really.'

'Someone said you'd hooked up with a rabbi.'

'Sort of.'

'Sort of hooked, or sort of rabbi?'

Titch and Levi made an odd couple, standing in the bright sunshine. Apart from the obvious difference in stature, Levi's clothes, though similar in style, were well worn and distinctly faded. The greatest difference, though, was their posture. Titch was upright, alert, nervous; Levi was comfortable with himself and relaxed about the world around him. Titch glanced instinctively over both shoulders, checking who was around.

'Have you heard of Jesus from Nazareth?' Levi asked in response to Titch's question.

'The miracle worker?'

Levi winced slightly at his friend's choice of words. 'There's a bit more to it than that.'

Genuine shock began to creep over Titch's neatly shaven face. 'Have you sold out to that working class populist preacher?' His prejudices underlined every word.

'Not sold out, no.'

Half an hour later, the two men were still there: Levi sitting on the ground, Titch on a rock protruding from the wall. Levi had finished telling his story – a story he had told many times during the past two years.

Titch listened, fascinated to hear how a man so much like himself had abandoned all the perks of the Roman Empire in favour of what Levi called the 'Empire of God'.

'Don't you ever regret it?' Titch asked.

Levi laughed. 'Maybe… when I'm trying to get some sleep in a cave that smells of sheep pee, with only my faded Roman coat for warmth.' He lifted the hem of the coat in question. 'That's when I remember what it was like to share a soft bed with a beautiful woman.'

Titch's eyes widened and his head dipped slightly, asking for more. These were the details that interested him.

Levi disappointed him. 'No. If I could go back again to the moment when Jesus walked into my office and asked me to join him, I'd do it all again.'

'All?' Titch was eager to extract some small regret from the former collector of taxes.

'OK … maybe one regret,' Levi conceded, soberly.

Titch smiled in triumph.

'I wish I had spent less time siphoning money from men and pouring it out on women, and instead found myself a decent, loving wife.'

Now Titch really was disappointed.

A new voice broke into their conversation. 'Well… Zacchaeus, my old adversary!'

Titch tightened instantly and swivelled his head round to the intruder. A dark-robed man was sauntering towards them.

Levi giggled quietly. 'Zacchaeus! Is that your real name?'

Titch was agitated by the intrusion. Then hastily, as the unwelcome visitor drew nearer, he added, 'I assume you're not really called Levi.'

'Matthew,' Levi replied. The tall man was now standing over them.

'Are you plotting some new crime, Zacchaeus? Or simply passing on the secrets of your evil trade?'

'It's not a trade, Josiah.' Their conversation had the feel of one that had been repeated many times. 'I provide an essential service to the security of our nation.'

'Why is it, then, that I never feel very safe around you?' the man mocked.

Titch glanced at Levi, reluctant to continue this verbal duel in the company of his friend.

Levi stood up. 'I don't think we've met before,' he said warmly, extending a welcoming hand towards the stranger.

Josiah did not return the compliment.

Titch stood too, though the top of his head was below the chins of both the other men. 'Josiah, this is Levi, an old friend of mine. Levi, Josiah is the chairman of the local synagogue and he owns most of the land you can see.'

'I am one of Zacchaeus' most productive customers,' the synagogue ruler added cynically. Looking at Levi's Roman coat, he added, 'You don't dress as a Levite.'

'It's a nickname,' Levi explained.

Titch contributed, 'We called him Levi for his religious tendencies.'

'I assume that it's money you worship, not God,' Josiah sneered.

'Josiah has been trying to convert me to his religion for years,' Titch told Levi.

'I've never attempted to convert anyone,' Josiah disclaimed. Then, half to himself, he added, 'It's not possible for a leopard to change its spots.'

Titch scratched his head. Then, mocking, said 'Why are we talking about wild cats all of a sudden?'

'Are you not a predator, Zacchaeus?' Josiah responded. 'Prowling around, looking for some poor man or woman to destroy?'

Before Titch could match the barb, Levi explained, 'It was a reference to the prophet Jeremiah, Titch. It means: once evil, always evil.'

Josiah was impressed. 'I rather hope, Zacchaeus, that you have been taking lessons from your friend here, and not the other way round.'

Titch grasped the opportunity. He climbed onto the rock on which he had been sitting, bringing his face almost level with the two taller men. 'Josiah,' he said pointedly, 'I would like you to meet a leopard who has, most certainly, changed his spots.'

Josiah looked quizzically at Levi, and then back to Titch.

'Levi, here, used to be my colleague in the unenviable task of raising contributions towards national security…'

'A tax collector,' Josiah stated bluntly.

Titch ignored him, continuing, '… but he has followed the calling of his nickname, and is training to become a rabbi.'

Josiah was impressed and interested. 'Who are you following?'

Titch was determined to score as many points against his old enemy as he could. 'No less a teacher than the rabbi of the moment, the people's favourite, the man of miracles and mystery…' (Titch did not know how effectively he was displaying his ignorance of current religious politics.) '… the Messiah from Nazareth, Jesus.'

Levi winced.

Josiah said, disappointed, 'Oh, him!'

It took some persuading, on Levi's part, for Titch and Josiah to follow him to the house where Jesus was staying. But years of experience of extracting taxes from reluctant landowners had equipped him well for the challenge. Josiah, for all his suspicion and prejudice, could not deny that Jesus appeared to have God on his side. As for Titch, he was ever so slightly unsettled by the idea that there might be something in the world more dependable than a large accumulation of Roman currency.

They did not walk together. Their route took them right through the town and Josiah had no desire to be associated with the two tax collectors in any way other than in being their victim; he walked several paces behind. As Levi strode across the thinning market square with Titch, he was reminded of the loneliness of his former occupation. Almost everyone they passed made a point of deliberately turning their backs on Titch. And the two of them were deliberately spat at on three occasions.

Titch responded with threats: 'I'll not forget that, next time we meet.' He meant it.

Levi wiped away the spittle and walked on. From time to time, he looked behind him to check that Josiah was still following. Though they had just met, Levi had warmed to the synagogue leader. Most Pharisees would simply not bother with a tax collector, but Josiah had evidently resolved never to give up his attempts to reform Titch.

Once clear of the town, Josiah caught up with them and the three men headed across the patchwork of fields and date plantations towards a small cluster of houses.

'Where are you taking us?' Titch asked Levi cautiously.

'My colleague Mary has an old friend who lives in the villa on the far right.'

Both Titch and Josiah had supplementary questions. Josiah began his a fraction before Titch. 'Are you suggesting that your Jesus has women disciples?'

'Sort of.'

Titch's question was, 'Levi, do you know what kind of a house that villa is?'

'I've got a fair idea.'

Levi's replies left his companions with a great deal to think about. They walked on in silence until Levi spoke again.

'How was the date harvest last year?' he asked Josiah innocently.

'*I* did reasonably well out of it,' Titch replied.

Josiah grunted contemptuously before expressing what was on his mind. 'I've often observed that women are more spiritually astute than men.'

They arrived at the cluster of houses. There was a wide spectrum of dwellings from the overly ornate villa Levi had pointed out, to a ramshackle shanty.

'I never even knew this little community was here,' Josiah said. It was only slowly dawning on him what kind of community this was.

'You wouldn't,' Titch observed, amused. 'They pay a fair contribution to the tax fund though, I can tell you.'

They were at the villa door, around which bloomed a red-flowering creeper.

'I'll find out where Jesus is,' Levi offered.

Josiah had finally reached some understanding. 'I can't go in there… into a brothel,' he exclaimed.

'Oh, come on, Josiah,' said Titch with a gleeful smile. 'No one's going to see. Anyway, we're here to meet a rabbi. I thought you approved of that sort of thing.'

'Yes, but I most certainly don't approve of this sort of thing.' He was sweating.

Levi disappeared inside, leaving the two antagonists with nobody to speak with but one another.

'Josiah,' Titch said, trying to take control of the situation. 'The ladies who work here are just… ordinary people doing their best to earn a living and care for their families. They aren't going to hurt you. Or infect you with evil. They are no different from you.'

Josiah swelled up with fury.

'I'll rephrase that,' Titch said quickly. 'They are little different from you. But they love their children; they want to be loved; they work hard. Are not those things just as true of you?'

Josiah gave a muted grunt, adding, 'I still can't go in.'

Titch was relishing the challenge before him. 'Josiah, would you not love it for me to come into your synagogue and willingly take part in the proceedings?'

The older man nodded very cautiously.

'I will do a deal with you. I am not asking that you take part in the usual proceedings of this establishment – I know that's against your religion – but if you will come in here and meet this man Jesus with me, then I will come to your synagogue every Sabbath for the next month.'

Josiah was tempted... not, of course, tempted by the reputation of the house, but by the prospect of getting Zacchaeus nearer to God.

Levi emerged. 'Jesus is in the parlour. Come in.'

Titch looked at Josiah.

Josiah fidgeted. 'I can't.'

'Can't what?' Levi asked.

Titch replied, 'He can't come in.'

'There's no need to worry,' Levi said naively. 'Everyone's just standing around listening to Jesus. There's nothing else happening.'

'It's not that... simple,' Josiah squirmed.

Titch explained. 'If he comes in, he is honour-bound to accept the hospitality of the household. And if he does that, then he is extending the hospitality of his own home to the people of this... place. And...' – here he could not restrain a grin – 'if all the ladies here were to turn up at Josiah's home expecting his wife to cook a meal for them, it might cause a little bit of a commotion in the synagogue.' He then looked proudly at Josiah. 'You see, I'm not nearly as stupid as you like to think I am.'

'I'll tell Jesus we have a problem,' Levi suggested.

'No, I'll just go home,' Josiah said, defeated.

'Please don't,' Levi begged. 'Wait a moment. I'll see what I can arrange.'

Titch and Josiah were left alone again. In fact, they were both uncomfortable about the situation. Titch was no less nervous of meeting a rabbi than Josiah was of meeting the ladies of the house.

Jesus appeared in the open doorway. He was shorter than Levi, robustly built, and wearing typical labourer's clothes. He extended a thick muscular arm towards Josiah and gripped the Pharisee's hand firmly.

'Josiah, it's a pleasure to meet you.' His pleasure was evident.

He extended the same roughly-clad arm towards Titch's manicured hand.

Titch had never before found himself sharing a greeting with a synagogue leader. He felt his hand squashed by the carpenter's grip, but the delight of the situation outweighed his pain.

'Zacchaeus, it's a pleasure to meet you.' Jesus' two greetings were equally balanced.

Titch, unusually, found himself feeling proud of his proper name. Usually it was only used against him, either by his mother or by Josiah.

Jesus held the two men in his gaze and announced, 'Matthew explained the problem. I suggest we decamp to the shade of that fig tree.' He pointed. 'Is that acceptable to you, Josiah?'

Josiah nodded.

'Titch?'

He smiled his acceptance.

A glorious assortment of people gathered under the fig tree. Jesus' disciples included four fishermen and two reformed terrorists. The local residents all seemed to be outlaws of one sort or another. However, there were two other Pharisees in addition to Josiah, one of whom Josiah knew well. There was even a centurion from the nearby Roman garrison. Apparently Jesus made no distinctions.

Titch and Josiah stood side by side in the circle around Jesus. He invited them both to ask a question.

Titch went first. He was in serious mood, which surprised him. Usually he enjoyed being irreverent when among religious people. 'Is it really true,' he asked, 'that I have to keep all the old laws of Moses if I am to avoid the fires of hell?'

'That is an excellent place to start,' Jesus began.

Josiah was greatly encouraged by this reply but resisted the smug smile he was tempted to give.

'But keeping laws will never be enough.'

Josiah's thoughts of a smile vanished.

'Unless your goodness is far greater than the goodness of these Pharisees,' Jesus told the tax collector, 'you will never have a right to enter heaven.'

All three Pharisees were now frowning. They had devoted their lives to keeping the ancient laws.

Titch looked up anxiously at Josiah. He had always been comfortable with his rejection of the Pharisee's strict morality. Jesus was moving the target and Titch was not sure whether to be pleased or concerned.

'The Law says, You must not commit adultery,' Jesus continued. This caused some nudging among the resident prostitutes. 'But what I'm telling you is that anyone who even looks at a woman or man lustfully, puts themselves in danger of hell.'

At this, Jesus looked searchingly into the eyes of every single person present.

Only Titch managed to meet his gaze for more than a moment. He knew that his lifestyle broke all the traditional moral codes and, up to that moment, the fact had never bothered him. He glanced from the prostitutes to the Pharisees and back again. It was hard to tell which of the groups was most embarrassed by Jesus' comment. It would have been an entertaining moment if he were not beginning to feel quite uncomfortable himself.

Jesus broke the silence with a clap of his hands.

'Josiah,' he beamed, 'what's your question?'

'I've just changed it,' the older man mumbled. It took him a few moments to compose his thoughts. Everyone was patient.

'If what you say is true,' the Pharisee said cautiously, 'how can any of us enter heaven?'

'It's impossible,' Jesus answered.

Josiah was not the only one to look confused. He shifted his feet awkwardly.

Jesus then added, 'But what is impossible with men, is possible with God. Let me tell you a story.'

At this suggestion most of the people present relaxed. Storytelling was a popular entertainment and Jesus was famous for his stories. Titch and Josiah, however, did not relax. They were both anxious to hear a satisfactory answer to their questions.

Levi smiled at the sight of two such different men, side by side, giving the same rapt attention to his rabbi.

Jesus began. 'There was a man who had two sons.'

Titch was immediately alert to the possibility that one of these sons might turn out to represent him. Josiah was listening with his head, not his emotions.

'The younger son,' the story continued, 'went to his father and said, *Dad, why should I wait for you to die before I enjoy my inheritance? Can I have my share of your estate now?* So the father divided his land between the two of them. And the younger son sold off his entire share, took the money, and left home.'

Jesus gave his audience time to soak in this shocking scenario. Josiah was frowning. Titch now had little doubt that he was this son Jesus was talking about.

'The young man headed for a distant city where he frittered away his wealth on wild living, until the day came that he had spent his last coin.'

Josiah was now nodding sagely, pleased to hear that the immoral fool had fallen on hard times.

'At that time,' Jesus went on, 'a severe famine struck that whole country. And the younger son had nothing. The only work he managed to find was feeding pigs.'

Even Titch was revolted by this. Only the centurion's face was free of disgust at the suggestion.

Jesus resumed: 'So there the young man sat, starving to death in a strange place, surrounded by pigs which were far better fed than him.'

Titch was sobered. It was a miserable end for a once happy and wealthy man. Jesus' story had touched on the very fear which made him get up and go to work every morning. He felt great sympathy for this younger son.

'Eventually the man came to his senses. What was he doing, starving to death, in a foreign country, when his father's staff were all well paid and well fed? *I will go back to my father,* he resolved, *and I will say, Father, I have wronged heaven and I have wronged you. I do not deserve to be called your son; please employ me as a member of your staff.* So the young man got up, and returned home.'

Josiah was shaking his head mournfully. It was a pointless plan. After bringing such disgrace on his family, the younger brother's life would have been safer among the hated pigs.

'It was a long and lonely journey.' Jesus' audience listened with rapt attention. 'But while he was still some distance from home, his father saw him and recognised him. The old man ran down the road to greet his son and threw his arms around him and kissed him. The son was ready with his speech: *Father, I have wronged heaven and I have wronged you. I do not deserve to be called your son, please employ me...* He never finished. The father led him by the hand into the house and called out to his staff. *Quick!* he said, *Get some decent clothes on him. Put the family ring on his finger and some shoes on his feet. And let's have a party to celebrate. Spare no expense!*'

Josiah could not believe it. He muttered crossly to himself, 'It would never happen.'

Titch, however, was now smiling. He liked the thought of the party. No rabbi he had ever heard ended a parable with an extravagant party.

But the story did not end there.

'The older son,' Jesus continued, 'was working out in the fields when his brother arrived. When he came home that evening and heard music and dancing, and smelt the roasting ox, he asked what was happening. *Your brother has come back,* someone told him, *and your father has put on a party to welcome him home.* The older son was furious, and refused to have anything to do with the event.'

Again Josiah nodded. To reward such outrageous behaviour was irresponsible. But out of the corner of his eye he noticed Titch looking up at him. It was not at all the practised disinterest the tax collector usually reserved for him. Their eyes met.

Jesus was continuing his story. 'The father heard about this and went out to meet his older son. He begged him to join in the celebrations. But the son said, *Look! I've been slaving away for you all these years, and what have I ever done to upset you? Yet you've never even given me a small goat so I could have a party with my friends. But when this son of yours comes sauntering home after squandering your property on prostitutes – YOU KILL THE FATTED CALF FOR HIM!*'

Jesus' voice had risen to a frantic pitch. He held everyone's attention. Josiah's mind was poised, balanced on the knife-edge of the narrative. His prejudice had been laid bare and he felt as though everyone in the circle was looking directly at him, even though he could see that they were all looking at Jesus.

'*My son,* the father said,' and now Jesus' voice was calm and tender, '*you have always been with me, and everything I own is yours.*'

Josiah was startled to find himself still loved. A moment earlier he had feared the worst for the elder son.

Jesus resumed the father's reply. '*It is right that we celebrate today, because this brother of yours was lost and is now found; he was dead and is alive again!*'

TO TRAP A RABBI

AZEL HAD BEEN looking forward to his encounter with Jesus. It was an opportunity to prove himself. The governing council's religious lawyers, based in Jerusalem, had sent him to question the unorthodox rabbi before the troublesome teacher and his ragtag bunch of associates arrived in the Holy City for the Passover festival.

Azel was not the first to be given this task. The Council had sent a long line of representatives in recent years. Initially, the Council had seen the popular rabbi from Nazareth as inconsequential. Most of the people living in the northern territories were considered a little strange. So they sent a series of junior and newly qualified lawyers to investigate reports of the wine-loving, party-going rabbi with a penchant for storytelling. But, one by one, these young men had returned, humbled and defeated by the uneducated carpenter. Now, with the annual festival fast approaching, sending Azel represented a change in strategy. Jesus presented a serious threat to national unity; the experienced mind of a senior lawyer was required.

Two years earlier there had been a succession of letters from anxious officials whose synagogues had been visited by the law-breaking teacher. This Jesus didn't appear to take Jewish law seriously. In fact, he deliberately flouted it. And he was particularly quick to disregard the most spiritual of their ancient laws: the command to avoid work on the Sabbath day. This Jesus, this low-caste carpenter, delighted in healing people on the Sabbath and, as any physician would agree, healing people was work.

Jesus' teaching methods were also a cause for concern. He told stories, as did many rabbis. But his were unspiritual stories... stories of the common life... silly stories. The people lapped them up. The opinions of other provincial rabbis were divided. Was this Jesus a blessing or a curse? He was certainly filling the synagogues; he wasn't engaged in any violence or racketeering, as far as they could tell. But was his message orthodox? They were not sure. He always refused to explain his stories.

So the experts from Jerusalem were called in. Azel had seen them leave, one after another, full of confidence. And then, two or three weeks later, he had seen them return, as bemused and muddled as the old men who ran the village synagogues around Galilee.

This anxiety had gone on for nearly two years. Then everything went quiet. Jesus had travelled north, out of their reach and concern, with just a small group of followers. He was no longer addressing large rallies on the hillsides around the Sea of Galilee. He was no longer performing apparent miracles right under the lawyers' noses. He was gone. The complaints stopped, and other matters quickly filled the minds of the Temple lawyers.

But Azel had not forgotten Jesus. He quietly harboured a desire to meet the man, to take him on in open debate, to probe his weak points, to point out his hypocrisy. For Azel had studied religion for long enough to know that all religious leaders conceal at least one major hypocrisy somewhere in the complex of their opinion and practice.

From time to time, Jesus had turned up in Jerusalem for major festivals. He would settle himself in one of the quiet colonnades round the edge of the Temple precincts and hold court for a few days. He didn't attract the vast crowds that flocked around him in Galilee. Jerusalem Jews were more sophisticated. They weren't so easily impressed with stories about kings and shepherds.

Jesus' visits were always carefully monitored by members of the Council. Numbers of Azel's colleagues tried to engage him in debate, but the Galilean wonder-rabbi never gave a straight answer to a simple question.

Azel watched, pondered and waited. He knew his turn would come, eventually. He wouldn't make the same mistakes that his colleagues had. He would be less aggressive, less direct; he would ease his way into Jesus' confidence and then uncover the fundamental flaw in the man's thinking. There had to be a flaw. Jesus was too good to be true. His healings and miracles were obviously a diversion, like the tricks a magician uses to distract his audience's gaze at the key moment. Jesus' renunciation of wealth and power were, no doubt, a cover for some plot to undermine the existing order and then seize power in yet another tedious peasants' revolt. There was nothing new under the sun.

Azel had been content to wait.

Now his time had come. Jesus was marching on Jerusalem with an unprecedented number of Galilean pilgrims. There was talk about him proclaiming himself as king. He was, apparently, a legitimate descendant of the ancient kings of Israel. Detailed plans were being drawn up in Jerusalem to defuse the threat Jesus posed, and Azel had been sent as a high-level scout to discern his intentions.

Of course, Azel would carry out the investigation requested by his superiors. But he also had his own agenda. He knew what was waiting for Jesus in

Jerusalem. But if he, Azel, could deliver the killer blow single-handedly and lay bare Jesus' weakness or fraud, the reward in terms of influence and reputation would be considerable.

Azel arrived at the Galileans' travelling camp the night before – tired, dusty and relieved. (The road from Jerusalem, following a deep gorge carved into the Judean wilderness, was not one that anyone was advised to travel alone.) A few polite enquiries led him to the place where Jesus and his followers were sleeping, and he flopped down nearby, resting his aching limbs. There were no indications of the gathering military force which had been rumoured: the main group seemed to be just thirteen men of assorted ages snoring under their travel blankets around a faltering fire.

Azel didn't sleep much. He lay awake planning for the morning… for his confrontation with Jesus.

At first light, the sound of hungry children and short-tempered parents quickly filled the air. Azel watched as Jesus rolled up his blanket and gathered a few marauding youngsters to tell them a story or two while their parents assembled some breakfast. Word that the rabbi was teaching spread around the encampment. Soon there was a fair-sized crowd standing around the former carpenter. Azel found himself a space at the edge, self-conscious among so many northern peasants, but nonetheless proud of his distinctive lawyer's robes. He waited patiently for the right moment to put his first question to Jesus.

Jesus finished his story: some nonsense about an unscrupulous servant commended for cheating by his master. This was Azel's moment. He raised an arm. 'Teacher! Teacher!'

Jesus noticed Azel, but chose to take a question from one of the children at the front. It was very frustrating. Azel was glad his colleagues in Jerusalem couldn't see him being forced to take second place to a bunch of kids.

He struggled to stay calm. Jesus was doing this deliberately. Jesus knew well enough that there was a senior lawyer from the Temple wanting to question him. Azel dressed in the customary robes of his profession, unlike Jesus, who dressed like a builder…

He was telling another story, about an idiot shepherd who lost one sheep and abandoned ninety nine others in order to find it. It was a preposterous tale, like most of Jesus' parables. Azel had heard it before. He and his colleagues had spent many an evening trying to uncover the secret messages in Jesus' tales, as reported back by those who had investigated the man. Not even a shepherd would be stupid enough to throw a party for his friends while ninety nine of his sheep were still wandering, uncared for, around the open countryside. Azel remembered something one of his fellow lawyers had said: 'The man's obsessed with parties.'

The people loved it. Azel could see it on their faces. He studied those faces intently and wondered what Jesus was really doing to them while he enchanted them with these mindless fables.

'In the same way,' Jesus concluded, 'there will be more celebration in heaven over one sinner who turns back to God, than over ninety nine good people...'

Azel missed the rest. Anger flooded his mind. Jesus was at it again – undermining the law, suggesting that sinners were more important than God-fearing people. He felt equally angry at the ignorant Galilean pilgrims for their unquestioning loyalty to Jesus. *These people are so stupid!* he shouted within the confines of his own mind. *We go out of our way to give them honest, responsible, disciplined leadership and they hate us for it. But Mr Party from Nazareth turns up, sinks a few drinks with them and they think they've found the Messiah.*

Jesus had finished. Azel fixed his gaze on the rabbi's irritating smile. His hand shot up. 'Teacher! Teacher!'

This time Jesus returned his gaze. The smile did not waver. Jesus rewarded the eminent lawyer with exactly the same display of teeth he had given to the children.

'No respect!' Azel muttered to himself through barely moving lips. He remembered a saying of his late father: Never trust a smiling Samaritan. *Actually*, he pondered, momentarily distracted from the task in hand, *I'm not sure I've ever seen a smiling Samaritan. They're a grim lot.* He noticed that Jesus was still smiling broadly and it unnerved him.

'Teacher...'

Azel noted that his voice had raised a few tones without his permission. He was nervous. Why should he be nervous? Theological debate was what he excelled at; he had made a career of it. He had debated Jewish law with high priests, with Roman governors and eastern mystics, even with his opposite number in the abominable temple at Samaria. There was no good reason for being nervous of a storytelling carpenter, even if he was a direct descendant of King David.

'Teacher...' Jesus was listening attentively, Azel's moment had arrived. 'What must I do to inherit eternal life?'

That was his angle of attack: come across as a genuine enquirer. His colleagues had been too aggressive. Everyone wants to be liked, especially a would-be messiah. Anyway, it was a fair question, one frequently debated within the walls of the Temple, and he knew that eternal life was a consistent theme in Jesus' stories.

Jesus looked intently into Azel's eyes. Azel was prepared for that. Almost all his failed colleagues had reported that Jesus seemed to know what they were thinking. That, Azel knew, was a confidence-sapping trick. He was not going to fall for it. He maintained his aspect of serious enquiry; that's what people expected from lawyers.

However, Jesus' searching gaze did make Azel feel self-conscious. Finally, 'What is written in the Scriptures?' Jesus asked the lawyer.

Azel was ready for that. Jesus often replied to questions with a counter-question. Many lesser lawyers had been disarmed by this tactic. But Azel had studied all the reports written about Jesus and knew the answer that the teacher had himself given to that question on more than one occasion.

He gave the impression of careful thought.

Jesus gently prompted him. 'What do you think?'

Azel's reply was measured. 'Love the LORD your God with all your heart…' He could see immediately that Jesus was pleased by his choice. '… and with all your soul, and with all your strength…' Jesus was nodding in agreement; so were his followers. This was going well. '… and with all your mind.'

He had hit his target. He had drawn Jesus in. He decided to embellish his reply with a little carefully considered detail. 'And…' Jesus was eagerly waiting for what came next. Azel was not nervous any more. He was on home territory; this was his specialist subject. 'And… love your neighbour as yourself.'

He allowed his lips to form a small smile while he waited for Jesus to reply.

'You are quite right,' Jesus said in his thick northern working-class accent.

This brought a much broader smile to Azel's mind, but he did not let it spread to his face. His long wait and meticulous preparation were paying off. He must not ruin his advantage by displaying petty prejudice.

Jesus was still smiling that same smile with which he taught the children. Azel should, perhaps, have resisted its charm. But his defences were temporarily lowered. He could not prevent himself from wanting Jesus' genuine approval. Just for a moment he was dazzled by the carpenter's affirmation.

Without a hint of suspicion or political guardedness, Jesus said to Azel, 'Do this and you will live.'

Azel snapped back into his professional mindset. He started to panic inside: *Hey, wait a minute, country carpenter! Don't go thinking I've come here looking for your advice. I'm the one with the theological qualifications out of the two of us.*

His pride went on the offensive. Months – no, years – of cold deliberation momentarily succumbed to fear that he might be thought soft or sycophantic.

'Teacher?' he said, ensuring that there was a firm edge to his voice. He wanted a debate, not a smiling pat on the back. He fumbled mentally for a counter question. 'Who is my neighbour?'

That regained the initiative. There were as many answers to that question as there were lawyers in Jerusalem. Jesus could answer it without realising that Azel was a threat.

Jesus shifted his posture, causing everyone in the small crowd to turn round and look at him. They settled themselves, expecting that he was about to tell another story.

Azel listened attentively. He did not want to lose the initiative. He wanted everyone – especially Jesus – to know that this story was for his benefit and that he reserved the right to ask some supplementary questions when it was over.

Jesus began: 'A man was going down from Jerusalem to Jericho...'

The very road Azel had walked on the previous day! Jesus would have known that. It was also the road that Jesus' audience would be climbing as soon as they had finished their breakfast. *Very clever!* Azel observed silently.

Jesus continued: '... and he fell into the hands of robbers.'

It was a notorious route. Azel knew at least three lawyers who had been mugged on that road in the last year. It was one of the drawbacks of wearing lawyers' robes.

'They stripped him of his clothes, beat him up and went away...'

Azel attempted to block the image from his thoughts. As soon as he'd finished with Jesus, he would have to take the same road back. There was no alternative – except though Samaritan territory, and that was even more dangerous for a Jew.

Jesus continued this depressing scene: '... leaving him half-dead.'

Poor man! Azel couldn't help being drawn into the narrative. One of his own teachers had been the victim of this very crime and had limped ever since. Did Jesus know that? It seemed unlikely. But Azel reminded himself that this Jesus was a highly dangerous and manipulative leader.

'It so happened that a priest was going down the same road...'

Fortunate, Azel pondered. Faces all around him brightened at this good news.

'When the priest saw the man lying there...'

I don't really see the point of this. Anyone would...

'... he walked past on the other side.'

Azel was hit by the emotional blow. He was a priest too – many lawyers were – and Jesus was looking directly at him with a searching look. Azel was thrown on his back foot. *Hey! Don't look at me like that,* he wanted to shout at the storyteller. *I've never ignored a neighbour in need. Never.* He had no reason to feel guilty under Jesus' gaze, but he did. He knew that not all priests were committed to a life of thoroughgoing honesty.

Jesus' face was inscrutable. His eyes were locked on to Azel's. 'Next, a Levite came to the place where the man lay, and saw him.'

This time Jesus appeared to pause deliberately. Azel had time to prepare an imagined defence for whatever this fictional Levite might do.

Jesus' tone of voice was sober, solemn even. 'He also walked by on the other side of the road.'

Azel knew that Jesus was firing this story directly at him. He glanced hurriedly around the faces in the crowd. They knew it too, and were rather enjoying the sport. *You're a fool, Jesus,* his mind raced. *I came here because I was prepared to work with you. There are others who would sooner have you killed.*

Jesus shifted position, sitting taller. The story was about to take another twist. 'Then a Samaritan…'

A Samaritan! The mention of the Jews' hated enemy caused an uncomfortable stir throughout the audience. The Galileans had even more reason to despise the Samaritans than did those who lived in and around Jerusalem.

Jesus waited for the murmur to die down, then repeated, 'A Samaritan, as he travelled, came where the man was.'

Azel had stopped wondering about Jesus' strategy; he could not prevent himself from feeling sorry for the victim who, having already lost so much, was about to lose his very life to an unnamed Samaritan scum.

Why didn't the Levite help him? Azel couldn't help wondering. I suppose he feared that the man wasn't really injured but a decoy put there by thieves. Or perhaps he had already spotted the Samaritan. He fought to regain control of his own thoughts. He had to concentrate. He would have to respond to the story as soon as it ended, before Jesus could turn back to the children.

'And when the Samaritan saw the man, he took pity on him.'

Azel coughed in disbelief. It just came out. He regretted it, but he couldn't stop it. A wave of distaste crashed over him as he remembered he would have to give a full report of this hateful story to the Jewish Council.

Jesus hadn't finished. 'The Samaritan,' he explained, 'went to the man and bandaged his wounds, pouring on oil and wine.'

Azel was impatient now for Jesus to get to his punchline. Many of his parables were comic; this one was abhorrent.

Jesus cast his eyes around the confused faces in front of him, returning his attention to Azel. 'Then…' he said dramatically.

Azel did not want the pause. In his imagination, he filled in his own conclusion to the tale: *Then the robbers jumped on the Samaritan and beat him up. Which only serves him right for interfering in other people's…*

He stopped himself. He regained his composure. He struggled to think like a lawyer. The wretched story had subverted his mental discipline. He hated the Samaritans more than he hated the Romans. The Romans were barbaric, but the Samaritans were evil.

Jesus was moving on. 'Then the Samaritan put the injured man on his own donkey…'

This is getting ludicrous!

'… brought him to a guest house…'

No Samaritan would do that for a Jew.

'… and took care of him. The next day, the Samaritan counted out two days' wages and gave them to the owner. He said, Look after him and when I return

I will reimburse you for any extra expense you may have.'

Treasonable tosh!

Jesus had finished.

Azel was shocked. He ran his mind hurriedly back over the story. The Samaritan had been good. The priest and the Levite had failed. What was Jesus trying to tell him? Could Jesus have struck up an alliance with the Samaritans? There was no evidence that he had.

Jesus was looking straight into Azel's eyes. There wasn't the slightest trace of a smile on his face now. Azel felt extremely uncomfortable; and he knew that Jesus had intended that discomfort. A few minutes earlier, Azel had felt so confident that he would succeed where others had failed, but Jesus' story had slipped through his mental armour. He had no idea what the story meant; he only knew that he felt insulted, guilty and defeated.

'Which of these three…' Jesus was asking the question and making it quite clear that he expected an answer. He was still looking directly at Azel. 'Which of these three, do you think, acted as a neighbour to the man who fell into the hands of robbers?'

Azel's only hope of succeeding in his mission involved him giving the right answer to this question. And the right answer could not be the one that Jesus was expecting. His mind raced around a hundred possibilities but always ended up at the same place. The answer to Jesus' question was blindingly obvious.

Azel had been trapped.

'It was… the… er…'

He checked himself. *I'm not saying 'the Samaritan.' If I do, and these Galileans don't lynch me, my colleagues in Jerusalem certainly will.*

Jesus held the same patient, uncompromising expression.

Azel weighed his options. There was only one way forwards. 'It was the… er… the one who had… who had mercy on him.'

Everyone was looking at him. His peripheral vision picked up the sea of faces: amused, intrigued, smiling, scowling, accepting, hostile. He could not quite believe that he had just publicly praised a Samaritan. He hoped the people had noted he had not actually said the 'S' word. He longed for Jesus to say something, to turn this unwelcome attention away from him.

Jesus' eyes did not move from Azel. Azel returned the gaze. He was a laywer, experienced at hunting for betrayal in people's faces. There was none in Jesus. There was no trace of arrogance or hatred, no delight in victory, no thrill of the contest. Before those eyes, Azel felt as he had on the rare occasions when his father had given him genuinely undivided attention. It was disconcerting, coming from a Galilean construction worker twenty years his junior.

Calmly, quietly and without the faintest hint of gloating, Jesus said to Azel, 'Go and do the same.'

A MATTER OF DEATH OR DEATH

'Arrrhhhhh!'

Pain. Agony. Sharp, stinging, searing, tearing shock.

There had been plenty of time to prepare himself: while they marched him through the barracks; while they pulled off his clothes – all his clothes; while they tied his wrists to rusty iron rings, suspending naked flesh against rough stone. Plenty of time to prepare his mind, to remember all he had ever been told about the Roman lash: thin leather straps studded with shards of broken bone. Plenty of time, as they rammed a filthy lump of wood between his teeth, to imagine what thirty nine lashes would actually feel like. But no amount of imagined pain – even when you can see the instrument of torture carelessly dropped at your feet – prepares you for the real thing.

The pain of the first stroke was too much: the stinging, the cutting, the bruising, the tearing, the scratching – all in a moment. But there was no time to adapt, no time to think. Before he had finished his first agonised cry… another lash, another scream, another sickening pull of tearing flesh… another crack. His once healthy frame thrashed against unforgiving stone again and again. Each time, the bloody tendrils of the lash embraced his flesh – his shoulder, across his thighs, down his back. Then the straps were dragged away, resisting, holding onto him like terrified children to their mothers' legs, ploughing his skin in preparation for the sowing of yet another crop of leather and sharp bone.

Seasons of scientific abuse revolved with breathtaking speed. Someone was counting – yes, this was calculated brutality – but Jesus could not hear that voice over the cacophony of pain.

Before the onslaught began, Jesus had deliberately reminded himself not to be lured into hating his attackers. He needn't have bothered. His pain allowed no space for hatred. All he could do was hurt.

The agony was fading, rapidly fading. So was the dispassionate voice of the Roman soldier, methodically counting the blows. Everything was muffled. Nothing was real. He was slipping. All that remained was a high, whistling whine. Was this death? Was death this easy?

Then, blackness.

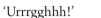

'Urrrgghhh!'

An invasion of consciousness. Cold wetness driving away blissful numbness. Throbbing… stinging… bruising… swelling… Jesus was slumped in the dirt. He had been cut down from the wall.

More water – blissfully cool, cruelly reviving. He sucked it into his mouth, salty from sweat and blood. When had he last drunk? He struggled to remember. Not since last evening; a lifetime ago. Last evening he had been a free man, he had eaten the annual Passover meal with his friends. He had told them what was going to happen. He remembered their blank, frightened faces when he had talked to them of arrests, trials and beatings.

That was the beating, then. No, that was one of the beatings. His memory was reviving. There had also been the punching, laughing Temple guards. That had been more humiliation than pain, quite different from the flogging. Sometimes people died from the flogging; Jesus remembered being told that. He had survived.

Strong hands grabbed him, pulling him up. They delivered him to his feet and left him there, legs straddled, swaying to keep himself steady as if on a small boat in a storm. He had done that once, a long time ago. But now the storm was within and its waves were of nausea and pain. He managed to stay upright. A victory! To be able to stand after all that! His mother would be proud of him. But there was no one to share his triumph. Where was his mother? Somewhere in the city.

Jesus looked at the Roman soldiers through blurred eyes. He had seen Roman soldiers all his life; he had got to know a few; he had once healed the son of a Roman soldier. But these were different; rough men splattered with blood – his blood – and they were laughing.

Jesus remembered laughter. He had done plenty of laughing over the years, before… before last night. He had laughed at all kinds of things with all kinds of people. The religious leaders had taken his laughter very seriously. They didn't think that God was a laughing matter. But they didn't know God.

What were these Romans laughing at? Surely, there could be nothing funny about the wreckage of a man who had just been flogged. It was something else.

Jesus forced his eyes into focus. They were laughing at him… at his head… at something he couldn't see on his head.

There was blood trickling down his face. Warm blood. He tasted it. When did he last have a drink? He had already asked himself that. But he was so thirsty… He was so thirsty, yet they were laughing at him. Why? They had put something on his head, and they thought it was very funny.

Another soldier strode forwards. He was holding something purple – Roman purple. It was a length of purple cloth. The soldier draped the cloth around Jesus' naked shoulders. The laughter doubled. The soldier stepped back and looked at him, grinning boyishly. Jesus looked at that grin. He had grinned once – a long time ago – before last night.

The soldier saluted him. It was a mocking salute. 'Hail, King of the Jews.' A roar of hilarity echoed round the courtyard. Jesus understood. The thing on his head was a crown of some sort… a crown that hurt badly.

Earlier… how much earlier he could not remember… but before the flogging, there had been a private interview with the Roman governor, a frightened and insecure man called Pontius something… he could not remember the name through the pain. They had discussed kingship. But it was a useless discussion. The governor did not want to understand. He just wanted Jesus to help him out of an awkward situation. Jesus had refused. He remembered the shapeless fear in the older man's eyes, a fear which had quickly turned to anger. Anger is easier to handle than fear, especially when you have several squadrons of Roman soldiers at your command. In his anger, Pontius whatever-his-name-was had sent Jesus for flogging. That's what you get for seeing a Roman governor's fear.

The soldier who had brought the purple robe still stood in front of Jesus. They searched each other's faces for a moment, struggling to understand one another across chasms of unbelievable pain and institutional loathing.

The soldier was not afraid, nor angry. He was bored. Bored… and something else. Jesus looked into the man's eyes, seeing something he had seen in countless eyes – Greek, Jew, Samaritan – throughout his life, something that frequently accompanied the routine brutality of the human race: a desire – no, a need – to impress others.

The eyes snapped away from Jesus' gaze. The man's feet shuffled in the dirt, his chin dropped to his chest and… THWACK! He smashed Jesus across the cheek.

———

The Jewish priests bayed like hyenas when they saw Jesus being guided towards them, draped in imperial purple and crowned with sharp thorns. They were delighted and horrified at the handiwork of the despised Romans. Jesus looked at them. They were like plumped-up cushions, in their fancy robes. He had told them how ridiculous they looked. The priests were harder to love than the Romans. Jesus understood that they thought they were right. They wholeheartedly believed that they were defending the work of God. In fact, they were often destroying the work of God. He had told them so, and he had told everyone else so. Back then, Jesus knew they were planning to kill him, but he didn't stop. He didn't stop telling the truth. The work of God cannot stop for petty plots and proud priests.

'The work of God' – he couldn't have expected that it would feel like this. 'The work of God' always seemed so strong… a guiding light, an unshakeable principle. 'The work of God' had motivated Jesus through every struggle and tussle of his life. It was so much more real to him than the stone and wood of the Temple, than the antique scrolls of the synagogue or the ancient traditions of his people.

'The work of God.' What was it? What did it mean now? Standing when the pull of gravity is almost too strong to resist? Looking into the eyes of the man who has just split your lip, and still not hating him? Accepting the punishment of those pompous priests because that is what their law requires? What was it to do the work of God? To die? Last night – all that time ago – it seemed so obvious. Now, nothing was obvious. Human life was a tangled complexity of…

Panic surged uninvited through Jesus' body. Death! A tangled complexity of death. How much worse could it get?

Last night in the garden, before they arrested him, the prospect of death was terrifying. He only just managed to keep himself from running away. And now, standing queasily in the morning sun, blood dripping onto his dusty feet, ears filled with self-righteous jeers, the brutal reality of life had already exceeded his expectations. Death was still to come.

He looked around the enclosed world of the Roman governor's residence. What was happening?

Nothing.

That was awful.

It's hard to see 'nothing' as the work of God.

~

The sound of studded Roman sandals emerged from the palace behind him. Relief. Anything is easier than nothing.

A voice: 'Here he is.'

It was Pontius, the governor. Governor Pilate – yes, that was his name. He was talking to the high priests, who were quiet and looking past Jesus. Pilate's voice was slightly strangled, a touch too high. Fear again. Afraid of the priests. Jesus scanned the faces of the priests. They were no less afraid. What a mess! Everyone was afraid. Well, not the soldier – the one who'd hit him. He wasn't afraid.

'Look at the man,' Pilate entreated the white-robed priests. 'He is no danger to anyone. I find no basis for a death sentence.'

A dozen pairs of dark Jewish eyes fixed on Jesus. What must he look like? Bloody, torn flesh.

Whatever those educated eyes saw, it still frightened them.

'Crucify him!'

It was a familiar voice.

'Crucify him!'

Several voices at once.

'Crucify him!'

A muddle of overlapping sounds.

Another wave of panic swept through Jesus. Up to that moment, crucifixion had only been an idea… a real idea, a present idea, but only an idea. Now it was a reality, a dreaded cocktail of pain and humiliation just as real as the flogging. No. More so. The flogging had taken only a handful of minutes. Crucifixion would take as many hours… or even days. He had seen it happen.

The baying priests were silenced.

In the moment of quiet there was just time to think, 'The work of God…'

'If you want him dead, kill him yourselves.'

Pilate again… a little more confident now. 'As for me, I can see no reason for it.'

The chief priest stepped forward. Jesus saw him puffing himself up like a turkey. It hurt the chief priest's pride to rely on cooperation from the Roman governor. The Jewish leaders were not allowed to do executions. Legalised death was the exclusive province of the Romans. They were expert at it.

'According to our law, this man has to die.'

Jesus struggled through a fog of exhaustion to fix his mind on the chief priest's words. His mind was reluctant. When did he last sleep? He had spent most of last night being punched and kicked by the chief priest's personal guards.

'He must die, because he claimed to be the Son of God.'

There was a snort of derision. Pilate? Or one of his henchmen?

Jesus' spirit slumped within his harrowed body. On another day he might have snorted himself. The words echoed through the muffled chambers of his mind. He must die, because he claimed to be the Son of God. The priest was quite right. It was a terrible thing to claim to be God. All too many people had tried it across humanity's sordid history. It always led to disaster. You had to have a law against it.

Footsteps. Pilate's footsteps. For a fleeting moment Jesus wondered how he knew that. Then the man was right in front of him… as close as the soldier had been. He looked into the governor's eyes. No, it was not Pilate who had snorted. Pilate was terrified.

The governor said nothing. There were too many thoughts in his head. He marched away, out of sight, away from Jesus. The footsteps stopped. Lowered voices. What was he saying? It mattered so much. Jesus needed to hear. This was a matter of life or death. They were talking in Latin. He couldn't understand. He so much wanted to understand, to be in control of his destiny – 'the work of God.'

Jesus stopped himself. It was not a matter of life or death. That was vanity. It was a matter of death or death. The chief priests would not let him live. He'd made sure of that. He'd made certain of that two days ago in the crowded Temple, when he told everyone just what he thought of the chief priests and their pompous religion.

Strong hands grabbed him. His body resisted. His mind didn't; it was his body that was stuck. How long had he been standing there? The dry blood cracked as he was forced to walk, following the diminishing form of Pontius Pilate into the Roman palace.

Inside: dark, cool, quiet.

Pilate was waiting for him. Legs apart, arms folded. He was resolved to sort this out, once and for all. The Jewish priests were a threat; this ragged rabbi was a nuisance. Jesus could see it all in the Roman's face.

'Where do you come from?'

Stupid question! How many honest answers were there to that? Jesus said nothing.

'Do you refuse to answer me?'

Jesus studied the army of messages written on the rich Roman's face. He did not need to say anything; to say nothing was to answer, 'yes'.

Pilate grew more agitated.

For a moment, Jesus imagined this powerful man having lunch with his beautiful Roman wife in a few hours' time. There was a shocking normality about that imagined scene. What would they talk about over their meal while he – Jesus – was being crucified? Would Pilate mention him? Probably not.

That thought stung as much as the lash had.

Pilate's head tilted to one side. He was trying to understand the silent stranger in his home.

'Don't you realise that I have authority to free you or to crucify you?'

'You would have no authority over me, if it had not been passed down to you from above.'

Jesus observed a fraction of relief in the man. He had won a reply. But when Pilate tried to understand what had been said, the relief was gone. His brow creased deeply.

Jesus continued. 'The one who handed me over to you, he has the greater guilt.'

The governor was not prepared for such ideas. He had been expecting a rebel or a madman, or a fanatic. He was not ready to consider the origins of authority and the relativity of guilt. He spun round and returned to the bloodthirsty priests.

Jesus waited in the cool silence. It had been good, for a brief time, to consider deeper matters. Now his body was seizing up again, there was a deep throbbing in his back, from his neck down to his knees. He felt faint. He leaned back against a cold stone pillar.

'Owwwwwhhhhh!'

He jerked himself forwards.

How long will it hurt? he wondered.

He answered himself: Don't be stupid. You're going to die.

Jesus turned and looked at the pillar. So much blood! His blood.

Jesus wanted to pray for Pontius Pilate as the execution detail herded him out of the palace gate and into the claustrophobic streets of Jerusalem. It was only right that he should. He had taught, so many times, that his fellow Jews should pray for the occupying Romans. That was 'the work of God', to pray for your enemies. But to pray for someone else you have to reach beyond yourself. And it's difficult to reach beyond a thick wooden plank that's been laid across your bleeding and lacerated back.

Jesus stopped in the palace gateway. In the few seconds before the blunt end of a Roman spear shunted into his side, he prayed that the governor might have a peaceful lunch with his beautiful wife. He breathed in the city air; his head felt clearer. Something indefinable had lifted his spirits.

As he stepped forward again, the weight of the heavy cross-beam shifted on his raw shoulder. The agony – momentarily – was total. He resolved that, if he could help it, he would not stop again before this final walk was complete. But it would not be so.

Less than an hour before, simply keeping his battered body upright had been a triumph. Now, to carry such a weight so far at the efficient pace of the Roman army was not possible. Jesus collapsed. He simply folded. For the second time in one morning, he was a heap of flesh and bone in the dry dust of Jerusalem. He was shivering. Not from fear. From shock. It had been a relief to hear Pontius Pilate finally proclaim, 'Let him be crucified.' No more uncertainty. No more politics.

Or maybe it was not just shock that made him shiver. Yes, Jesus was afraid… very afraid.

The heavy beam was lifted from him, allowing him to breathe – something he had not been able to do against its weight. That piece of wood would kill him. He noted the irony. For eighteen years, he had made his living carrying lengths of wood. He had been a carpenter. He realised now what had lifted his mood. The smell of the wood! For all the pain of carrying such a load on his tortured back, some indefinable comfort had come from that familiar smell. It was the scent of carefree childhood days spent helping his stepfather Joseph in the family workshop.

Firm hands pulled Jesus to his feet. He wanted to retreat into the cocoon of his childhood memories. He made himself look at the faces around him. They were ugly, every one. Fear and pain do not leave space for beauty. In some faces he saw raw hatred. It was the other faces that drained his soul… those that showed only disinterest or disappointment. Could they be right? Was it possible that he was about to die for nothing? Might he, just like the priests, have misunderstood 'the work of God'?

Jesus was jabbed forwards, made to walk. Where was his cross, the instrument of his death, his oddly comforting piece of wood? A total stranger, an African, had been conscripted to carry it for him. Jesus' passions raged. How dare they give away his piece of wood? How dare they conclude that he was not capable of carrying it? He fought these instincts. He caught the African's eye. He wanted to thank him. He tried, but he couldn't. He could only walk.

A small rise in the road ahead towered over him like a craggy mountain top. It seemed impossible that anyone could climb such a peak. Jesus bullied his mind into remembering the jumbled Galilean hills among which he had spent most of his life. There was a time when he would have bounded up this little slope with ease. It was hard to imagine. For the last quarter of a mile, every single step had been a work of supreme effort. Just to drag one foot in front of the other, just to keep his balance, just to shift his weight from one foot to the other, took all his thought. Yet he was determined to climb that hill. He had chosen to die. This was 'the work of God'. There was nothing more important than to conquer that wretched hill and face death of his own free will.

The man carrying his cross-beam walked past him. The shaggy form of a prison-rotted human followed; he too was carrying a cross. Then another. So, there were three of them scheduled to die. The implications of that discovery tore savagely at Jesus. To die alone and abandoned by his own people was 'the work of God'. He had accepted that. But to die with these… these criminals… was not how he had imagined it. It was as if the occupying Romans were dispensing with some rotten wood from their timber pile.

Halfway up that pathetic hill, the truth engulfed Jesus like a mudslide. He too was no more than some rotten wood that needed to be cut out and destroyed… a job he himself had done many times, back in his carpentry days, a lifetime ago.

A familiar Roman face stopped beside him. It was the soldier who had hit him. Jesus did not wait to be shoved. He dragged a foot forward, pressed it down, shifted his weight onto it, hauled the other past it up the slope, pressed that down… actions so complex, so essential, that it allowed no mental space for anything else – except, perhaps, for a little love… love for the Roman soldier. In one small crevice of his mind, Jesus thanked God that the man had not hit him twice.

How long had it taken him to climb that slope? Time had slowed so much that it no longer seemed to move at all. A wide, featureless desert separated him from the moment of his death. He watched as one of his fellow victims collapsed, exhausted. Jesus wished he had the energy to do the same, but he didn't dare upset the precarious equilibrium that was holding him where he was. To fall so far, to move so fast, was unimaginable.

The soldier pushed him.

Oh, he could do it after all. For a timeless moment there was the exhilaration of weightlessness, and the relief for his legs of no longer holding his body upright. Then the sickening, grating, crunching landing on the insensitive verge beside the road.

He couldn't move. His cheek pressed into sharp gravel, his dry mouth was full of dust, the thorns in his makeshift crown burrowed deeply into his skull.

Not all pains are alike. There is the pain of having the clothes ripped off your back, opening up your wounds in the process. There is the pain of having those open wounds filled with splinters as you are dragged over rough, unplaned wood. The pain of having a large nail hammered through your right hand – your working hand – is quite different from that of having your left hand nailed to thick dark wood. Some pains make you gasp, others make you curse. His two fellow victims were doing a lot of that. Jesus stared into the eyes of the man causing all these pains. He cared. It was comforting to see that he did. The soldier cared that he did a good job. Jesus thanked God that the man cared, and prayed for forgiveness for him. It was not this man's fault that Jesus was about to die… well, no more than it was the fault of every other person in the world.

In all the chaos of noise and torture, accompanied by the contrasting curses of executioners and condemned men, Jesus caught a whiff of a familiar smell. A homely smell. Not the smell of wood or hammer or nails. It was a deeper, older, more reassuring scent. But the memory was quickly erased when the soldiers hauled the heavy cross upwards, dragging Jesus' inert frame with it.

He watched his own legs as they swayed independently below him. He felt strangely disconnected from his own existence. Was this death? Was he moving beyond pain?

CRASH!

'Ougggghhh!'

No, he wasn't.

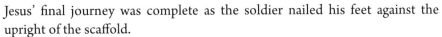

Jesus' final journey was complete as the soldier nailed his feet against the upright of the scaffold.

Now, he thought to himself when that surge of pain had subsided, I am like a piece of wood fixed to an item of furniture.

There was no pleasure in that thought. Only despair. He was no longer human. Just a bit of stuff nailed to another bit of stuff, because someone wanted it there.

He did not want to open his eyes. Wood cannot see.

He battled to breathe warm air into his lungs. It hurt.

He wasn't just a piece of stuff. Not yet.

After several agonising breaths Jesus began to get the hang of it. He had to push himself up on his nailed feet – which hurt – so that his body swayed forward, away from the woodwork, suspended on the nails in his hands – which hurt – and then take a deep breath – which also hurt – before slumping exhausted, allowing the iron restraints in his hands and feet to hold him for a while as the hard-won air leaked slowly out of his lungs.

As he grew accustomed to this procedure, it was possible to take several breaths, pushed up on agonised feet, before his muscles gave way.

It was then that Jesus caught the scent again. He did not know what it was, but it made him cry. Hot tears pushed out from behind his tight-closed eyelids. His thoughts were no longer keeping to the established patterns of memory or logic; they wandered haphazardly around his mind, bumping into long-forgotten impulses. That smell caused a tangle of associations in his fading consciousness, and that tangle informed him: 'You are loved.'

Hanging between breaths, Jesus opened his eyes. There were the crow-like priests, waiting for their carrion. There were the soldiers, playing dice for the right to keep his clothes. There were the disinterested and the disappointed, for whom this whole 'work of God' had been devised. And there... there just below him, her face flooded with tears, was his mother.

He had to breathe. It would hurt, but it had to be done.

How odd that after a week of resolutely driving the Jewish leaders into having him killed, he should now be driving his body to stay alive. He could not die yet... not just yet. First he had to speak to his mother. She had suffered so much for him over the years: ridicule, anguish, incomprehension. And now this. He had to speak to her. He had to show her that he loved her.

Love. Wasn't that why he was here? Wasn't that 'the work of God'? Yet it is hard to love when you are in agony. Every impulse urges you to preserve yourself. Jesus pushed himself up for more breaths. He was here for 'the work of God' which was love – he knew that. He was here not to survive; that was selfish. He was here to die. But first he had to love his mother.

He hauled himself up for a few more snatched breaths. His friend was there – John the fisherman. Dear John… John who loved him too.

He wrestled his wandering eyes to catch his mother's gaze. It wasn't hard. Her eyes were fixed on his. 'Woman,' he gasped, 'he is your son.' Jesus tore his attention away from his mother's and directed it towards his dear friend. 'John,' he said. 'She is your mother.'

He resolved not to push himself up for any more breaths. They were pointless; they were selfish.

But life, selfish life, fought back, hanging on for its own sake.

'I'm thirsty.'

He hadn't intended to say it out loud. His body had simply done it. He heard the scuffle of soldiers moving. He watched as they soaked a sponge in vinegar, stuffed it on the end of a long spear and held it up to his parched lips.

When had he last had a drink? He couldn't remember… couldn't remember much at all. His brain was almost all fog now. He remembered his mother's love, and the smell of her. He remembered the love of his true Father. It was clear: 'the work of God' was to give himself.

The drink was pointless. The drink was getting, not giving. 'The work of God' was to give.

The fog was thickening.

Even that last truth was being engulfed.

The world was going dark.

His mind was going dark.

The last thing to go in a dying man is his hearing.

As all thought, all understanding, all meaning, faded into nothingness, Jesus heard his own voice, muffled by a sponge.

It said: 'It's done.'

'Hmmmmmm!'

Darkness: cool darkness.

A smell: the smell of earth.

Quiet: total quiet.

A single drip, in the darkness. Water. Life.

Fingers: moving, feeling. Warm fingers in the cool darkness, feeling their own hand.

A hand: a familiar hand. The same hand that those fingers had always been attached to. Yet different. There was a hole, a deep hole, in it. And in the other hand, too.

A memory: a clear, distant, vital memory – 'That must be from the nails.'

Feet: checking, shuffling in the darkness. Toes prodding. Yes. Holes there, too.

A thought: a phrase, a command, an echo from beyond time. 'Let there be life.'

And there was life – a new beginning.

A smile: unseen in the darkness… cheeks bunched, lips pulled, teeth uncovered. And, with the smile, a memory: 'I have smiled before.'

Jesus stood up… well, crouched. You don't get standing room inside a tomb.

Did he speak the words that launched creation? Let there be light! We do not know.

But an angel appeared and rolled away the solid stone door, and there was light: the soft light of early morning.

Soldiers sprawled on the path outside, white with terror of the quaking ground and shining angel.

Jesus looked at their fallen strength. Any familiar faces among them? No.

Then, voices: women's voices, grief-laden, drained of emotion, approaching the tomb uncertainly.

Time to go. The angel had work to do.

Jesus left the angel to deliver his message. He walked away from his tomb, unseen, along the garden path, feeling the morning breeze.

Were his limbs stiff from dying and death? We do not know.

A little way along the path, Jesus was alone again. Alone and alive. Waiting.

Did he see the women rush past, alight with the angel's message? He waited.

Did he see his good friends, John and Peter, hurrying to the tomb some time later, to confirm the women's report? Did he see their muddled faces as they ambled back towards Jerusalem with empty news of an empty tomb? Did he see into their empty, confused hearts?

He was waiting, alone and alive. Waiting for something. Waiting for someone.

Returning to the scene of his burial, Jesus found who he was waiting for: young Mary. Not Mary, his mother, but Mary from Magdala… Mary who had suffered so much, who had been forgiven so much, who had loved so much… Mary who was crying so much.

She had been there on the Friday, at the place called Golgotha; she had watched him die. She had stayed there with Mary his mother and with John.

Now she was staying again, staying near his tomb.

She was waiting too, waiting out of a hope stronger than thought, stronger than doubt, as strong as love.

Jesus was smiling.

Mary was crying.

'Dear woman,' he asked, 'why are you crying?'

Mary dried her sodden eyes and glanced around. Glanced, but did not look. So she didn't see.

'They have taken away my master,' she sobbed. 'I don't know what they've done with him.'

She wiped her eyes again, eyes red from days of weeping and wiping. 'Is this your garden, sir?' she asked the stranger. 'Do you know where he is? If you do, please tell me.'

Jesus looked down at his grief-stricken friend. Grief is like pain; you can't think straight. He knew a lot about pain.

Then his smile widened as he considered the unimagined joy that he was about to bring to Mary's death-ridden heart. How good it felt to be smiling again!

The smile coloured his voice as he called his friend by her name, a name that he had spoken a thousand times: 'Mary.'

She caught her breath. The voice speaking her name echoed through her memories: *Mary, let me show you this… Mary, can you pass the bread? … Mary, we will be leaving in the morning … Mary, you are forgiven.*

Excitement raced through her body and mind. She spun round. She looked up. She looked and saw. She looked and understood. She looked and believed. She looked and spoke.

'Teacher!'

MUST KNOW STORIES – THE BIBLE ACCOUNTS

ADAM AND EVE – GENESIS
TO KNOW OR NOT TO KNOW

The Lord God formed the man from the dust of the ground and breathed into his nostrils the breath of life, and the man became a living being.

Now the Lord God had planted a garden in the east, in Eden; and there he put the man he had formed. And the Lord God made all kinds of trees grow out of the ground – trees that were pleasing to the eye and good for food. In the middle of the garden were the tree of life and the tree of the knowledge of good and evil...

The Lord God took the man and put him in the Garden of Eden to work it and take care of it. And the Lord God commanded the man, 'You are free to eat from any tree in the garden; but you must not eat from the tree of the knowledge of good and evil, for when you eat of it you will surely die.'

The Lord God said, 'It is not good for the man to be alone. I will make a helper suitable for him.'

Now the Lord God had formed out of the ground all the beasts of the field and all the birds of the air. He brought them to the man to see what he would name them; and whatever the man called each living creature, that was its name. So the man gave names to all the livestock, the birds of the air and all the beasts of the field.

But for Adam no suitable helper was found. So the Lord God caused the man to fall into a deep sleep; and while he was sleeping, he took one of the man's ribs and closed up the place with flesh. Then the Lord God made a woman from the rib he had taken out of the man, and he brought her to the man.

The man said,
'This is now bone of my bones
    and flesh of my flesh;
she shall be called "woman",
    for she was taken out of man.'

The man and his wife were both naked, and they felt no shame.

Now the serpent was more crafty than any of the wild animals the Lord God had made. He said to the woman, 'Did God really say, "You must not eat from any tree in the garden"?'

The woman said to the serpent, 'We may eat fruit from the trees in the garden, but God did say, "You must not eat fruit from the tree that is in the middle of the garden, and you must not touch it, or you will die."'

'You will not surely die,' the serpent said to the woman. 'For God knows that when you eat of it your eyes will be opened, and you will be like God, knowing good and evil.'

When the woman saw that the fruit of the tree was good for food and pleasing to the eye, and also desirable for gaining wisdom, she took some and ate it. She also gave some to her husband, who was with her, and he ate it. Then the eyes of both of them were opened, and they realised that they were naked; so they sewed fig leaves together and made coverings for themselves.

Then the man and his wife heard the sound of the LORD God as he was walking in the garden in the cool of the day, and they hid from the LORD God among the trees of the garden. But the LORD God called to the man, 'Where are you?'

He answered, 'I heard you in the garden, and I was afraid because I was naked; so I hid.'

And he said, 'Who told you that you were naked? Have you eaten from the tree from which I commanded you not to eat?'

The man said, 'The woman you put here with me – she gave me some fruit from the tree, and I ate it.'

Then the LORD God said to the woman, 'What is this you have done?'

The woman said, 'The serpent deceived me, and I ate.'

So the LORD God said to the serpent, 'Because you have done this,

Cursed are you above all the livestock
       and all the wild animals!
You will crawl on your belly
       and you will eat dust
       all the days of your life.
And I will put enmity
       between you and the woman,
       and between your offspring and hers;
he will crush your head,
       and you will strike his heel.'
To the woman he said,
'I will greatly increase your pains in childbearing;
       with pain you will give birth to children.
Your desire will be for your husband,
       and he will rule over you.'
To Adam he said, 'Because you listened to your wife and ate from the tree about which I commanded you, "You must not eat of it,"'

Cursed is the ground because of you;
       through painful toil you will eat of it all the days of your life.
It will produce thorns and thistles for you,
       and you will eat the plants of the field.
By the sweat of your brow

you will eat your food
until you return to the ground,
   since from it you were taken;
for dust you are
   and to dust you will return.'

Adam named his wife Eve, because she would become the mother of all the living.

The LORD God made garments of skin for Adam and his wife and clothed them. And the LORD God said, 'The man has now become like one of us, knowing good and evil. He must not be allowed to reach out his hand and take also from the tree of life and eat, and live for ever.' So the LORD God banished him from the Garden of Eden to work the ground from which he had been taken.

Genesis 2:7–25; 3:1–23

NOAH'S ARK – GENESIS
IN THE DARK

Noah was a righteous man, blameless among the people of his time, and he walked with God. Noah had three sons: Shem, Ham and Japheth.

Now the earth was corrupt in God's sight and was full of violence. God saw how corrupt the earth had become, for all the people on earth had corrupted their ways. So God said to Noah, 'I am going to put an end to all people, for the earth is filled with violence because of them. I am surely going to destroy both them and the earth. So make yourself an ark of cypress wood; make rooms in it and coat it with pitch inside and out. This is how you are to build it: The ark is to be 450 feet long, 75 feet wide and 45 feet high. Make a roof for it and finish the ark to within 18 inches of the top. Put a door in the side of the ark and make lower, middle and upper decks. I am going to bring floodwaters on the earth to destroy all life under the heavens, every creature that has the breath of life in it. Everything on earth will perish. But I will establish my covenant with you, and you will enter the ark – you and your sons and your wife and your sons' wives with you. You are to bring into the ark two of all living creatures, male and female, to keep them alive with you. Two of every kind of bird, of every kind of animal and of every kind of creature that moves along the ground will come to you to be kept alive. You are to take every kind of food that is to be eaten and store it away as food for you and for them.'

Noah did everything just as God commanded him.

... Noah was six hundred years old when the floodwaters came on the earth. And Noah and his sons and his wife and his sons' wives entered the ark to escape the waters of the flood. Pairs of clean and unclean animals, of birds and of all creatures that move along the ground, male and female, came to Noah and entered the ark, as God had commanded Noah. And after the seven days the floodwaters came on the earth.

In the six hundredth year of Noah's life, on the seventeenth day of the second month – on that day all the springs of the great deep burst forth, and the floodgates of the heavens were opened. And rain fell on the earth for forty days and forty nights.

On that very day Noah and his sons, Shem, Ham and Japheth, together with his wife and the wives of his three sons, entered the ark ... Then the LORD shut him in.

For forty days the flood kept coming on the earth, and as the waters increased they lifted the ark high above the earth. The waters rose and increased greatly on the earth, and the ark floated on the surface of the water. They rose greatly on the earth, and all the high mountains under the entire heavens were covered... Every living thing that moved on the earth perished – birds, livestock, wild animals, all the creatures that swarm over the earth, and all mankind... Only Noah was left, and those with him in the ark.

The waters flooded the earth for a hundred and fifty days.

But God remembered Noah and all the wild animals and the livestock that were with him in the ark, and he sent a wind over the earth, and the waters receded. Now the springs of the deep and the floodgates of the heavens had been closed, and the rain had stopped falling from the sky. The water receded steadily from the earth. At the end of the hundred and fifty days the water had gone down, and on the seventeenth day of the seventh month the ark came to rest on the mountains of Ararat. The waters continued to recede until the tenth month, and on the first day of the tenth month the tops of the mountains became visible.

After forty days Noah opened the window he had made in the ark and sent out a raven, and it kept flying back and forth until the water had dried up from the earth. Then he sent out a dove to see if the water had receded from the surface of the ground. But the dove could find no place to set its feet because there was water over all the surface of the earth; so it returned to Noah in the ark. He reached out his hand and took the dove and brought it back to himself in the ark. He waited seven more days and again sent out the dove from the ark. When the dove returned to him in the evening, there in its beak was a freshly plucked olive leaf! Then Noah knew that the water had receded from the earth. He waited seven more days and sent the dove out again, but this time it did not return to him.

By the first day of the first month of Noah's six hundred and first year, the water had dried up from the earth. Noah then removed the covering from the ark and saw that the surface of the ground was dry. By the twenty-seventh day of the second month the earth was completely dry.

Then God said to Noah, 'Come out of the ark, you and your wife and your sons and their wives. Bring out every kind of living creature that is with you – the birds, the animals, and all the creatures that move along the ground – so they can multiply on the earth and be fruitful and increase in number upon it.'

So Noah came out, together with his sons and his wife and his sons' wives. All the animals and all the creatures that move along the ground and all the birds – everything that moves on the earth – came out of the ark, one kind after another…

Then God said to Noah and to his sons with him: 'I now establish my covenant with you and with your descendants after you and with every living creature that was with you – the birds, the livestock and all the wild animals, all those that came out of the ark with you – every living creature on earth. I establish my covenant with you: Never again will all life be cut off by the waters of a flood; never again will there be a flood to destroy the earth.'

And God said, 'This is the sign of the covenant I am making between me and you and every living creature with you, a covenant for all generations to come: I have set my rainbow in the clouds, and it will be the sign of the covenant between me and the earth. Whenever I bring clouds over the earth and the rainbow appears in the clouds, I will remember my covenant between me and you and all living creatures of every kind. Never again will the waters become a flood to destroy all life. Whenever the rainbow appears in the clouds, I will see it and remember the everlasting covenant between God and all living creatures of every kind on the earth.'

Genesis 6:9–22; 7:6–24; 8:1–19; 9:8–16

THE TEN COMMANDMENTS – EXODUS
ORDER FROM CHAOS

In the third month after the Israelites left Egypt … they came to the Desert of Sinai … they entered the Desert of Sinai, and Israel camped there in the desert in front of the mountain.

Then Moses went up to God, and the LORD … said, 'This is what you are to say to the … people of Israel: "You yourselves have seen what I did to Egypt, and how I carried you on eagles' wings and brought you to myself. Now if you obey me fully and keep my covenant, then out of all nations you will be my treasured possession. Although the whole earth is mine, you will be for me a kingdom of priests and a holy nation."'

So Moses went back and summoned the elders of the people and set before them all the words the LORD had commanded him to speak. The people all responded together, 'We will do everything the LORD has said.' So Moses brought their answer back to the LORD.

The LORD said to Moses, 'I am going to come to you in a dense cloud, so that the people will hear me speaking with you and will always put their trust in you.' Then Moses told the LORD what the people had said.

And the LORD said to Moses, 'Go to the people and consecrate them today and tomorrow. Have them wash their clothes and be ready by the third day, because on that day the LORD will come down on Mount Sinai in the sight of all the people. Put limits for the people around the mountain and tell them, "Be careful that you do not go up the mountain or touch the foot of it. Whoever touches the mountain shall surely be put to death… " Only when the ram's horn sounds a long blast may they go up to the mountain.'

After Moses had gone down the mountain to the people, he consecrated them, and they washed their clothes. Then he said to the people, 'Prepare yourselves for the third day. Abstain from sexual relations.'

On the morning of the third day there was thunder and lightning, with a thick cloud over the mountain, and a very loud trumpet blast. Everyone in the camp trembled. Then Moses led the people out of the camp to meet with God, and they stood at the foot of the mountain. Mount Sinai was covered with smoke, because the LORD descended on it in fire. The smoke billowed up from it like smoke from a furnace, the whole mountain trembled violently, and the sound of the trumpet grew louder and louder. Then Moses spoke and the voice of God answered him.

The LORD descended to the top of Mount Sinai and called Moses to the top of the mountain. So Moses went up and the LORD said to him, 'Go down and warn the people so they do not force their way through to see the LORD...'

Moses said to the LORD, 'The people cannot come up Mount Sinai, because you yourself warned us, "Put limits around the mountain and set it apart as holy..."'

So Moses went down to the people and told them.

And God spoke all these words:

'I am the LORD your God, who brought you out of Egypt, out of the land of slavery.

'You shall have no other gods before me.

'You shall not make for yourself an idol in the form of anything in heaven above or on the earth beneath or in the waters below. You shall not bow down to them or worship them; for I, the LORD your God, am a jealous God, punishing the children for the sin of the fathers to the third and fourth generation of those who hate me, but showing love to a thousand generations of those who love me and keep my commandments.

'You shall not misuse the name of the LORD your God, for the LORD will not hold anyone guiltless who misuses his name.

'Remember the Sabbath day by keeping it holy. Six days you shall labour and do all your work, but the seventh day is a Sabbath to the LORD your God. On it you shall not do any work, neither you, nor your son or daughter, nor your manservant or maidservant, nor your animals, nor the alien within your gates. For in six days the LORD made the heavens and the earth, the sea, and all that is in them, but he rested on the seventh day. Therefore the LORD blessed the Sabbath day and made it holy.

'Honour your father and your mother, so that you may live long in the land the LORD your God is giving you.

'You shall not murder.

'You shall not commit adultery.

'You shall not steal.

'You shall not give false testimony against your neighbour.

'You shall not covet your neighbour's house. You shall not covet your neighbour's wife, or his manservant or maidservant, his ox or donkey, or anything that belongs to your neighbour.'

When the people saw the thunder and lightning and heard the trumpet and saw the mountain in smoke, they trembled with fear. They stayed at a distance and said to Moses, 'Speak to us yourself and we will listen. But do not have God speak to us or we will die.'

Moses said to the people, 'Do not be afraid. God has come to test you, so that the fear of God will be with you to keep you from sinning'...

Then he [the LORD] said to Moses, 'Come up to the LORD, you and Aaron, Nadab and Abihu, and seventy of the elders of Israel. You are to worship at a distance, but Moses alone is to approach the LORD; the others must not come near. And the people may not come up with him'...

Moses and Aaron, Nadab and Abihu, and the seventy elders of Israel went up and saw the God of Israel. Under his feet was something like a pavement made of sapphire, clear as the sky itself...

The LORD said to Moses, 'Come up to me on the mountain and stay here, and I will give you the tablets of stone, with the law and commands I have written for their instruction.'

Then Moses set out with Joshua his assistant, and Moses went up on the mountain of God. He said to the elders, 'Wait here for us until we come back to you. Aaron and Hur are with you, and anyone involved in a dispute can go to them.'

When Moses went up on the mountain, the cloud covered it ... To the Israelites the glory of the LORD looked like a consuming fire on top of the mountain. Then Moses entered the cloud as he went on up the mountain. And he stayed on the mountain forty days and forty nights.

When the people saw that Moses was so long in coming down from the mountain, they gathered round Aaron and said, 'Come, make us gods who will go before us. As for this fellow Moses who brought us up out of Egypt, we don't know what has happened to him.'

Aaron answered them, 'Take off the gold ear-rings that your wives, your sons and your daughters are wearing, and bring them to me.' So all the people took off their ear-rings and brought them to Aaron. He took what they handed him and made it into an idol cast in the shape of a calf, fashioning it with a tool. Then they said, 'These are your gods, O Israel, who brought you up out of Egypt.'

When Aaron saw this, he built an altar in front of the calf and announced, 'Tomorrow there will be a festival to the LORD.' So the next day the people rose early and sacrificed burnt offerings and presented fellowship offerings. Afterwards they sat down to eat and drink and got up to indulge in revelry.

Then the LORD said to Moses, 'Go down, because your people, whom you brought up out of Egypt, have become corrupt. They have been quick to turn away from what I commanded them and have made themselves an idol cast in the shape of a calf.' ...

Moses turned and went down the mountain with the two tablets of the Testimony in his hands. They were inscribed on both sides, front and back. The tablets were the work of God; the writing was the writing of God, engraved on the tablets...

When Moses approached the camp and saw the calf and the dancing, his anger burned and he threw the tablets out of his hands, breaking them to pieces at the foot of the mountain. And he took the calf they had made and burned it in the fire; then he ground it to powder, scattered it on the water and made the Israelites drink it...

The next day Moses said to the people, 'You have committed a great sin. But now I will go up to the LORD; perhaps I can make atonement for your sin.'

So Moses went back to the LORD and said, 'Oh, what a great sin these people have committed! They have made themselves gods of gold. But now, please forgive their sin' ...

The LORD said to Moses, 'Chisel out two stone tablets like the first ones, and I will write on them the words that were on the first tablets, which you broke. Be ready in the morning, and then come up on Mount Sinai...

So Moses chiselled out two stone tablets like the first ones and went up Mount Sinai early in the morning, as the LORD had commanded him; and he carried the two stone tablets in his hands...

Moses was there with the LORD forty days and forty nights without eating bread or drinking water. And he wrote on the tablets the words of the covenant – the Ten Commandments.

Exodus 19:1–25; 20:1–20; 24:1,2,9,10,12–15,17,18; 32:1–8,15,16,19,20,30–32; 34:1,2,4,28

DAVID AND GOLIATH – 1 SAMUEL
A SMALL, SMOOTH STONE

Now the Philistines gathered their forces for war and assembled at Socoh in Judah... Saul and the Israelites assembled and camped in the Valley of Elah and drew up their battle line to meet the Philistines. The Philistines occupied one hill and the Israelites another, with the valley between them.

A champion named Goliath, who was from Gath, came out of the Philistine camp. He was over nine feet tall. He had a bronze helmet on his head and wore a coat of scale armour of bronze weighing five thousand shekels; on his legs he wore bronze greaves, and a bronze javelin was slung on his back. His spear shaft was like a weaver's rod, and its iron point weighed six hundred shekels. His shield-bearer went ahead of him.

Goliath stood and shouted to the ranks of Israel, 'Why do you come out and line up for battle? Am I not a Philistine, and are you not the servants of Saul? Choose a man and have him come down to me. If he is able to fight and kill me, we will become your subjects; but if I overcome him and kill him, you will become our subjects and serve us.' Then the Philistine said, 'This day I defy the ranks of Israel! Give me a man and let us fight each other.' On hearing the Philistine's words, Saul and all the Israelites were dismayed and terrified.

Now David was the son of ... Jesse, who was from Bethlehem in Judah. Jesse had eight sons ... Jesse's three oldest sons had followed Saul to the war. David was the youngest. The three oldest followed Saul, but David went back and forth from Saul to tend his father's sheep at Bethlehem.

For forty days the Philistine came forward every morning and evening and took his stand.

Now Jesse said to his son David, 'Take this ephah of roasted grain and these ten loaves of bread for your brothers and hurry to their camp. Take along these ten cheeses to the commander of their unit. See how your brothers are and bring back some assurance from them.' ...

Early in the morning David left the flock with a shepherd, loaded up and set out, as Jesse had directed. He reached the camp as the army was going out to its battle positions, shouting the war cry. Israel and the Philistines were drawing up their lines facing each other. David left his things with the keeper of supplies, ran to the battle lines and greeted his brothers. As he was talking with them, Goliath, the Philistine champion from Gath, stepped out from his lines and shouted his usual defiance, and David heard it. When the Israelites saw the man, they all ran from him in great fear.

Now the Israelites had been saying, 'Do you see how this man keeps coming out? He comes out to defy Israel. The king will give great wealth to the man who kills him. He will also give him his daughter in marriage and will exempt his father's family from taxes in Israel.'

David asked the men standing near him, 'What will be done for the man who kills this Philistine and removes this disgrace from Israel? Who is this uncircumcised Philistine that he should defy the armies of the living God?'

They repeated to him what they had been saying and told him, 'This is what will be done for the man who kills him.'

When Eliab, David's oldest brother, heard him speaking with the men, he burned with anger at him and asked, 'Why have you come down here? And with whom did you leave those few sheep in the desert? I know how conceited you are and how wicked your heart is; you came down only to watch the battle.'

'Now what have I done?' said David. 'Can't I even speak?' He then turned away to someone else and brought up the same matter, and the men answered him as before. What David said was overheard and reported to Saul, and Saul sent for him.

David said to Saul, 'Let no one lose heart on account of this Philistine; your servant will go and fight him.'

Saul replied, 'You are not able to go out against this Philistine and fight him; you are only a boy, and he has been a fighting man from his youth.'

But David said to Saul, 'Your servant has been keeping his father's sheep. When a lion or a bear came and carried off a sheep from the flock, I went after it, struck it and rescued the sheep from its mouth. When it turned on me, I seized it by its hair, struck it and killed it. Your servant has killed both the lion and the bear; this uncircumcised Philistine will be like one of them, because he has defied the armies of the living God. The LORD who delivered me from the paw of the lion and the paw of the bear will deliver me from the hand of this Philistine.'

Saul said to David, 'Go, and the LORD be with you.'

Then Saul dressed David in his own tunic. He put a coat of armour on him and a bronze helmet on his head. David fastened on his sword over the tunic and tried walking around, because he was not used to them.

'I cannot go in these,' he said to Saul, 'because I am not used to them.' So he took them off. Then he took his staff in his hand, chose five smooth stones from the stream, put them in the pouch of his shepherd's bag and, with his sling in his hand, approached the Philistine.

Meanwhile, the Philistine, with his shield-bearer in front of him, kept coming closer to David. He looked David over and saw that he was only a boy, ruddy and handsome, and he despised him. He said to David, 'Am I a dog, that you come at me with sticks?' And the Philistine cursed David by his gods. 'Come here,' he said, 'and I'll give your flesh to the birds of the air and the beasts of the field!'

David said to the Philistine, 'You come against me with sword and spear and javelin, but I come against you in the name of the LORD Almighty, the God of the armies of Israel, whom you have defied. This day the LORD will hand you over to me, and I'll strike you down and cut off your head. Today I will give the carcasses of the Philistine army to the birds of the air and the beasts of the earth, and the whole world will know that there is a God in Israel. All those gathered here will know that it is not by sword or spear that the LORD saves; for the battle is the LORD's, and he will give all of you into our hands.'

As the Philistine moved closer to attack him, David ran quickly towards the battle line to meet him. Reaching into his bag and taking out a stone, he slung it and struck the Philistine on the forehead. The stone sank into his forehead, and he fell face down on the ground.

So David triumphed over the Philistine with a sling and a stone; without a sword in his hand he struck down the Philistine and killed him.

David ran and stood over him. He took hold of the Philistine's sword and drew it from the scabbard. After he killed him, he cut off his head with the sword.

When the Philistines saw that their hero was dead, they turned and ran.

1 Samuel 17:1–51

DANIEL IN THE LIONS' DEN – DANIEL
A MAN YOU CAN TRUST

That very night Belshazzar, king of the Babylonians, was slain, and Darius the Mede took over the kingdom, at the age of sixty-two.

It pleased Darius to appoint 120 satraps to rule throughout the kingdom, with three administrators over them, one of whom was Daniel. The satraps were made accountable to them so that the king might not suffer loss. Now Daniel so distinguished himself among the administrators and the satraps by his exceptional qualities that the king planned to set him over the whole kingdom. At this, the administrators and the satraps tried to find grounds for charges against Daniel in his conduct of government affairs, but they were unable to do so. They could find no corruption in him, because he was trustworthy and neither corrupt nor negligent. Finally these men said, 'We will never find any basis for charges against this man Daniel unless it has something to do with the law of his God.'

So the administrators and the satraps went as a group to the king and said: 'O King Darius, live for ever! The royal administrators, prefects, satraps, advisers and governors have all agreed that the king should issue an edict and enforce the decree that anyone who prays to any god or man during the next thirty days, except to you, O king, shall be thrown into the lions' den. Now, O king, issue the decree and put it in writing so that it cannot be altered – in accordance with the laws of the Medes and Persians, which cannot be repealed.' So King Darius put the decree in writing.

Now when Daniel learned that the decree had been published, he went home to his upstairs room where the windows opened towards Jerusalem. Three times a day he got down on his knees and prayed, giving thanks to his God, just as he had done before. Then these men went as a group and found Daniel praying and asking God for help. So they went to the king and spoke to him about his royal decree: 'Did you not publish a decree that during the next thirty days anyone who prays to any god or man except to you, O king, would be thrown into the lions' den?'

The king answered, 'The decree stands – in accordance with the laws of the Medes and Persians, which cannot be repealed.'

Then they said to the king, 'Daniel, who is one of the exiles from Judah, pays no attention to you, O king, or to the decree you put in writing. He still prays three times a day.' When the king heard this, he was greatly distressed; he was determined to rescue Daniel and made every effort until sundown to save him.

Then the men went as a group to the king and said to him, 'Remember, O king, that according to the law of the Medes and Persians no decree or edict that the king issues can be changed.'

So the king gave the order, and they brought Daniel and threw him into the lions' den. The king said to Daniel, 'May your God, whom you serve continually, rescue you!'

A stone was brought and placed over the mouth of the den, and the king sealed it with his own signet ring and with the rings of his nobles, so that Daniel's situation might not be changed. Then the king returned to his palace and spent the night without eating and without any entertainment being brought to him. And he could not sleep.

At the first light of dawn, the king got up and hurried to the lions' den. When he came near the den, he called to Daniel in an anguished voice, 'Daniel, servant of the living God, has your God, whom you serve continually, been able to rescue you from the lions?'

Daniel answered, 'O king, live for ever! My God sent his angel, and he shut the mouths of the lions. They have not hurt me, because I was found innocent in his sight. Nor have I ever done any wrong before you, O king.'

The king was overjoyed and gave orders to lift Daniel out of the den. And when Daniel was lifted from the den, no wound was found on him, because he had trusted in his God.

At the king's command, the men who had falsely accused Daniel were brought in and thrown into the lions' den, along with their wives and children. And before they reached the floor of the den, the lions overpowered them and crushed all their bones.

Then King Darius wrote to all the peoples, nations and men of every language throughout the land:

'May you prosper greatly!

'I issue a decree that in every part of my kingdom people must fear and reverence the God of Daniel...'

Daniel 5:30,31; 6:1–26

THE BIRTH AT BETHLEHEM – MATTHEW & LUKE
FAMILY POLITICS

God sent the angel Gabriel to Nazareth, a town in Galilee, to a virgin pledged to be married to a man named Joseph, a descendant of David. The virgin's name was Mary. The angel went to her and said, 'Greetings, you who are highly favoured! The LORD is with you.'

Mary was greatly troubled at his words and wondered what kind of greeting this might be. But the angel said to her, 'Do not be afraid, Mary, you have found favour with God. You will be with child and give birth to a son, and you are to give him the name Jesus. He will be great and will be called the Son of the Most High. The LORD God will give him the throne of his father David, and he will reign over the house of Jacob for ever; his kingdom will never end.'

'How will this be,' Mary asked the angel, 'since I am a virgin?'

The angel answered, 'The Holy Spirit will come upon you, and the power of the Most High will overshadow you. So the holy one to be born will be called the Son of God. Even Elizabeth your relative is going to have a child in her old age, and she who was said to be barren is in her sixth month. For nothing is impossible with God.'

'I am the LORD's servant,' Mary answered. 'May it be to me as you have said.' Then the angel left her.

Because Joseph ... was a righteous man and did not want to expose her to public disgrace, he had in mind to divorce her quietly.

But after he had considered this, an angel of the LORD appeared to him in a dream and said, 'Joseph son of David, do not be afraid to take Mary home as your wife, because what is conceived in her is from the Holy Spirit. She will give birth to a son, and you are to give him the name Jesus, because he will save his people from their sins.'

When Joseph woke up, he did what the angel of the LORD had commanded him and took Mary home as his wife. But he had no union with her until she gave birth to a son ...

In those days Caesar Augustus issued a decree that a census should be taken of the entire Roman world. (This was the first census that took place while Quirinius was governor of Syria.) And everyone went to his own town to register.

So Joseph also went up from the town of Nazareth in Galilee to Judea, to Bethlehem the town of David, because he belonged to the house and line of David. He went there to register with Mary, who was pledged to be married to him and was expecting a child. While they were there, the time came for the baby to be born, and she gave birth to her firstborn, a son. She wrapped him in cloths and placed him in a manger, because there was no room for them in the inn.

And there were shepherds living out in the fields near by, keeping watch over their flocks at night. An angel of the LORD appeared to them, and the glory of the LORD shone around them, and they were terrified. But the angel said to them, 'Do not be afraid. I bring you good news of great joy that will be for all the people. Today in the town of David a Saviour has been born to you; he is Christ the LORD. This will be a sign to you: You will find a baby wrapped in cloths and lying in a manger.'

When the angels had left them and gone into heaven, the shepherds said to one another, 'Let's go to Bethlehem and see this thing that has happened, which the LORD has told us about.' So they hurried off and found Mary and Joseph, and the baby, who was lying in the manger ...

After Jesus was born in Bethlehem in Judea, during the time of King Herod, Magi from the east came to Jerusalem and asked, 'Where is the one who has been born king of the Jews? We saw his star in the east and have come to worship him.'

When King Herod heard this he was disturbed, and all Jerusalem with him. When he had called together all the people's chief priests and teachers of the law, he asked them where the Christ was to be born. 'In Bethlehem in Judea,' they replied, 'for this is what the prophet has written:
"But you, Bethlehem, in the land of Judah,
    are by no means least among the rulers of Judah;
for out of you will come a ruler
    who will be the shepherd of my people Israel."'

Then Herod called the Magi secretly and found out from them the exact time the star had appeared. He sent them to Bethlehem and said, 'Go and make a careful search for the child. As soon as you find him, report to me, so that I too may go and worship him.'

After they had heard the king, they went on their way, and the star they had seen in the east went ahead of them until it stopped over the place where the child was. When they saw the star, they were overjoyed. On coming to the house, they saw the child with his mother Mary, and they bowed down and worshipped him. Then they opened their treasures and presented him with gifts of gold and of incense and of myrrh. And having been warned in a dream not to go back to Herod, they returned to their country by another route.

When they had gone, an angel of the LORD appeared to Joseph in a dream. 'Get up,' he said, 'take the child and his mother and escape to Egypt. Stay there until I tell you, for Herod is going to search for the child to kill him.'

So he got up, took the child and his mother during the night and left for Egypt, where he stayed until the death of Herod...

Luke 1:26–38; Matthew 1:19–21,24,25; Luke 2:1–12,15,16; Matthew 2:1–15

THE FEEDING OF THE 5000 – MARK & JOHN
AN IMPOSSIBLE REQUEST

The apostles gathered round Jesus and reported to him all they had done and taught. Then, because so many people were coming and going that they did not even have a chance to eat, he said to them, 'Come with me by yourselves to a quiet place and get some rest.' So they went away by themselves in a boat to a solitary place. But many who saw them leaving recognised them and ran on foot from all the towns and got there ahead of them. When Jesus landed and saw a large crowd, he had compassion on them, because they were like sheep without a shepherd. So he began teaching them many things.

By this time it was late in the day, so his disciples came to him. 'This is a remote place,' they said, 'and it's already very late. Send the people away so that they can go to the surrounding countryside and villages and buy themselves something to eat.'

But he answered, 'You give them something to eat.'

Philip answered him, 'Eight months' wages would not buy enough bread for each one to have a bite!'

'How many loaves do you have?' he asked. 'Go and see.' When they found out, they said, 'Five – and two fish.'

Then Jesus directed them to have all the people sit down in groups on the green grass. So they sat down in groups of hundreds and fifties. Taking the five loaves and the two fish and looking up to heaven, he gave thanks and broke the loaves. Then he gave them to his disciples to set before the people. He also divided the two fish among them all. They all ate and were satisfied, and the disciples picked up twelve basketfuls of broken pieces of bread and fish. The number of the men who had eaten was five thousand.

Mark 6:30–37; John 6:7; Mark 6:38–44

THE PRODIGAL SON – LUKE
THE PARABLE OF JOSIAH AND TITCH

Now the tax collectors and 'sinners' were all gathering round to hear Jesus. But the Pharisees and the teachers of the law muttered, 'This man welcomes sinners and eats with them.'

Then Jesus told them this parable:

'There was a man who had two sons. The younger one said to his father, "Father, give me my share of the estate." So he divided his property between them.

'Not long after that, the younger son got together all he had, set off for a distant country and there squandered his wealth in wild living. After he had spent everything, there was a severe famine in that whole country, and he began to be in need. So he went and hired himself out to a citizen of that country, who sent him to his fields to feed pigs. He longed to fill his stomach with the pods that the pigs were eating, but no one gave him anything.

'When he came to his senses, he said, "How many of my father's hired men have food to spare, and here I am starving to death! I will set out and go back to my father and say to him: Father, I have sinned against heaven and against you. I am no longer worthy to be called your son; make me like one of your hired men.' So he got up and went to his father.

'But while he was still a long way off, his father saw him and was filled with compassion for him; he ran to his son, threw his arms around him and kissed him.

'The son said to him, "Father, I have sinned against heaven and against you. I am no longer worthy to be called your son."

'But the father said to his servants, "Quick! Bring the best robe and put it on him. Put a ring on his finger and sandals on his feet. Bring the fattened calf and kill it. Let's have a feast and celebrate. For this son of mine was dead and is alive again; he was lost and is found.' So they began to celebrate.

'Meanwhile, the older son was in the field. When he came near the house, he heard music and dancing. So he called one of the servants and asked him what was going on. "Your brother has come," he replied, "and your father has killed the fattened calf because he has him back safe and sound."

'The older brother became angry and refused to go in. So his father went out and pleaded with him. But he answered his father, "Look! All these years I've been slaving for you and never disobeyed your orders. Yet you never gave me even a young goat so I could celebrate with my friends. But when this son of yours who has squandered your property with prostitutes comes home, you kill the fattened calf for him!"

'"My son," the father said, "you are always with me, and everything I have is yours. But we had to celebrate and be glad, because this brother of yours was dead and is alive again; he was lost and is found."'

Luke 15:1–3,11–32

THE GOOD SAMARITAN – LUKE
TO TRAP A RABBI

On one occasion an expert in the law stood up to test Jesus. 'Teacher,' he asked, 'what must I do to inherit eternal life?'

'What is written in the Law?' he replied. 'How do you read it?' He answered: '"Love the LORD your God with all your heart and with all your soul and with all your strength and with all your mind"; and, "Love your neighbour as yourself."'

'You have answered correctly,' Jesus replied. 'Do this and you will live.' But he wanted to justify himself, so he asked Jesus, 'And who is my neighbour?'

In reply Jesus said: 'A man was going down from Jerusalem to Jericho, when he fell into the hands of robbers. They stripped him of his clothes, beat him and went away, leaving him half-dead.

'A priest happened to be going down the same road, and when he saw the man, he passed by on the other side. So too, a Levite, when he came to the place and saw him, passed by on the other side.

'But a Samaritan, as he travelled, came where the man was; and when he saw him, he took pity on him. He went to him and bandaged his wounds, pouring on oil and wine. Then he put the man on his own donkey, brought him to an inn and took care of him. The next day he took out two silver coins and gave them to the innkeeper. "Look after him," he said, "and when I return, I will reimburse you for any extra expense you may have."

'Which of these three do you think was a neighbour to the man who fell into the hands of robbers?'

The expert in the law replied, 'The one who had mercy on him.'

Jesus told him, 'Go and do likewise.'

Luke 10:25–37

THE CRUCIFIXION OF JESUS – LUKE & JOHN
A MATTER OF DEATH OR DEATH

Then Pilate took Jesus and had him flogged. The soldiers twisted together a crown of thorns and put it on his head. They clothed him in a purple robe and went up to him again and again, saying, 'Hail, king of the Jews!' And they struck him in the face.

Once more Pilate came out and said to the Jews, 'Look, I am bringing him out to you to let you know that I find no basis for a charge against him.' When Jesus came out wearing the crown of thorns and the purple robe, Pilate said to them, 'Here is the man!'

As soon as the chief priests and their officials saw him, they shouted, 'Crucify! Crucify!'

But Pilate answered, 'You take him and crucify him. As for me, I find no basis for a charge against him.'

The Jews insisted, 'We have a law, and according to that law he must die, because he claimed to be the Son of God.'

When Pilate heard this, he was even more afraid, and he went back inside the palace. 'Where do you come from?' he asked Jesus, but Jesus gave him no answer. 'Do you refuse to speak to me?' Pilate said. 'Don't you realise I have power either to free you or to crucify you?'

Jesus answered, 'You would have no power over me if it were not given to you from above. Therefore the one who handed me over to you is guilty of a greater sin.'

From then on, Pilate tried to set Jesus free, but the Jews kept shouting, 'If you let this man go, you are no friend of Caesar. Anyone who claims to be a king opposes Caesar.'

When Pilate heard this, he brought Jesus out and sat down on the judge's seat at a place known as the Stone Pavement (which in Aramaic is Gabbatha). It was the day of Preparation of Passover Week, about the sixth hour.

'Here is your king,' Pilate said to the Jews.

But they shouted, 'Take him away! Take him away! Crucify him!'

'Shall I crucify your king?' Pilate asked.

'We have no king but Caesar,' the chief priests answered.

Finally Pilate handed him over to them to be crucified …

As they led him away, they seized Simon from Cyrene, who was on his way in from the country, and put the cross on him and made him carry it behind Jesus. A large number of people followed him, including women who mourned and wailed for him. Jesus turned and said to them, 'Daughters of Jerusalem, do not weep for me; weep for yourselves and for your children.'

Two other men, both criminals were also led out with him to be executed. When they came to the place called the Skull, there they crucified him, along with the criminals – one on his right, the other on his left. Jesus said, 'Father, forgive them, for they do not know what they are doing.' And they divided up his clothes by casting lots.

The people stood watching, and the rulers even sneered at him. They said, 'He saved others; let him save himself if he is the Christ of God, the Chosen One.'

The soldiers also came up and mocked him. They offered him wine vinegar and said, 'If you are the king of the Jews, save yourself.' …

Near the cross of Jesus stood his mother, his mother's sister, Mary the wife of Clopas, and Mary Magdalene. When Jesus saw his mother there, and the disciple whom he loved standing near by, he said to his mother, 'Dear woman, here is your son,' and to the disciple, 'Here is your mother.' From that time on, this disciple took her into his home.

Later, knowing that all was now completed, and so that the Scripture would be fulfilled, Jesus said, 'I am thirsty.' A jar of wine vinegar was there, so they soaked a sponge in it, put the sponge on a stalk of the hyssop plant, and lifted it to Jesus' lips. When he had received the drink, Jesus said, 'It is finished.' With that, he bowed his head and gave up his spirit.

Later, Joseph of Arimathea asked Pilate for the body of Jesus. Now Joseph was a disciple of Jesus, but secretly because he feared the Jews. With Pilate's permission, he came and took the body away. At the place where Jesus was crucified, there was a garden, and in the garden a new tomb, in which no one had ever been laid. Because it was the Jewish day of Preparation and since the tomb was near by, they laid Jesus there.

Early on the first day of the week, while it was still dark, Mary Magdalene went to the tomb and saw that the stone had been removed from the entrance. So she came running to Simon Peter and the other disciple, the one Jesus loved, and said, 'They have taken the LORD out of the tomb, and we don't know where they have put him!'

So Peter and the other disciple started for the tomb. Both were running, but the other disciple outran Peter and reached the tomb first. He bent over and looked in at the strips of linen lying there but did not go in. Then Simon Peter, who was behind him, arrived and went into the tomb. He saw the strips of linen lying there, as well as the burial cloth that had been around Jesus' head. The cloth was folded up by itself, separate from the linen. Finally the other disciple, who had reached the tomb first, also went inside. He saw and believed. (They still did not understand from Scripture that Jesus had to rise from the dead.)

Then the disciples went back to their homes, but Mary stood outside the tomb crying. As she wept, she bent over to look into the tomb and saw two angels in white, seated where Jesus' body had been, one at the head and the other at the foot.

They asked her, 'Woman, why are you crying?'

'They have taken my LORD away,' she said, 'and I don't know where they have put him.' At this, she turned round and saw Jesus standing there, but she did not realise that it was Jesus.

'Woman,' he said, 'why are you crying? Who is it you are looking for?' Thinking he was the gardener, she said, 'Sir, if you have carried him away, tell me where you have put him, and I will get him.'

Jesus said to her, 'Mary.' She turned towards him and cried out in Aramaic, 'Rabboni!' (which means Teacher).

Jesus said, 'Do not hold on to me, for I have not yet returned to the Father. Go instead to my brothers and tell them, "I am returning to my Father and your Father, to my God and your God."' Mary Magdalene went to the disciples with the news: 'I have seen the LORD!' And she told them that he had said these things to her.

John 19:1–16; Luke 23:26–28,32–36: John 19:25–30,38,41,42; John 20:1–18

ALSO BY ROBERT HARRISON

FOR ADULTS

THE ORIEL TRILOGY – three thought-provoking, humorous and insightful novels to take you inside and beyond the Bible text.

ORIEL'S DIARY – *An archangel's account of the life of Jesus*
The personal diary of Archangel Oriel, colleague of Gabriel and Michael, records the birth, life, death and resurrection of Jesus Christ. Closely based on Luke's Gospel, the book presents an entirely original view of a familiar story.

ORIEL'S TRAVELS – *An archangel's travels with St Paul*
From fanatical destroyer of the followers of Jesus to fearless gospel pioneer – the incredible story of the man central to the formation of the Church.

ORIEL IN THE DESERT – *An archangel's view of the life of Moses*
Archangel Oriel gives us the inside track on Moses, who rises from a dysfunctional family background to engage in the intrigue of Egyptian politics and who leads the escape from forced labour of the demoralised slaves destined to become God's chosen people.

FOR CHILDREN

THE STRONG TOWER
Beautifully illustrated in full colour by Roger Langton, this is a collection of stories to be read aloud or alone. With notes for carers to help children going through tough times.

Scripture Union publications are available from Christian bookshops, on the Internet, or via mail order. You can:

- phone SU's mail order line: 0845 0706006
- email info@scriptureunion.org.uk
- log on to www.scriptureunion.org.uk
- write to SU Mail Order, PO Box 5148, Milton Keynes MLO, MK2 2YX

Scripture Union
USING THE BIBLE TO INSPIRE CHILDREN, YOUNG PEOPLE AND ADULTS TO KNOW GOD